THE LEARNING BLOCK

By

Dr. Dean E. Grass

Manufactured in the United States of America

ISBN 0-930298-10-1

PREFACE

This modest volume attempts to make available to all teachers a new technique of mind conditioning that will make their efforts more successful. The contributors to this report want to pass on to all teachers a few of the many ideas and techniques they have developed through years of research and hard work. They agree that this publication is far from complete and that it does not contain answers to all the complex conditions or challenges that may be encountered in the days and years ahead. This book is an introduction to positive mind conditioning that describes the working of this new teaching technique. It is hoped that it will make the task of teaching easier, provide an insight regarding how the great human computer (the mind) is conditioned, how it should be conditioned and how it should *not* be conditioned, and the reasons why. The contributors hope that teachers will build upon and improve the techniques presented in this book.

It is sincerely hoped that the information contained herein will induce educators to continue the research we have begun. Far too many educators have turned their talents to finance, organization, testing, class-loads, etc.; very few recognize that the problem of education is mind conditioning. They have followed the psychologists who were not educators down many blind alleys; it is now high time that education steps out on its own and trains the gifted, the average, and the handicapped. It is essential that educators study the mind and how it is conditioned.

Special thanks are in order to the many teachers who

had the insight to try the methods and report on them and to the individual students who were willing and eager subjects in the research. A thank you to the members of the Phi Delta Kappa field chapter (Beta Psi) that took part in gathering material as well as parents of children who were very intelligent but who were not responding in school. These parents allowed their children to take part in the research. We are very grateful to the principals and guidance departments of our schools, who were willing to allow students to be conditioned with new ideas about their abilities and about how they should think; we also wish to acknowledge help received from research conducted by many educators in the field of the handicapped and gifted students. Their findings gave support to the theory and practiced described in this report.

The author wishes to thank two very wonderful persons for their patience and undersanding. Dr. F. C. McCormack for his technical advice, and Juanita Grass, the wife of the author, who gave hundreds of lonely hours over a period of years while he was working with students, attending meetings, and writing.

The prime statement made by Dr. R. C. McCormack, after he had reviewed the report, was "Everything you have written is true and has been known to scientists for a long time. Are you saying that education is so far behind time, that these concepts are not known by all teachers and are not being used in our schools?"

CONTENTS

INTRODUCTION

A New Theory of Learning

In recent years, the trend toward positive thinking and an appreciation of its advantages for those who use it have been rapidly increasing. Evidence of this advance becomes obvious as one reads new publications. Positive thinking had and continues to have a fundamental and constructive effect upon the lives of millions. Although the theory and practice of this kind of thinking have never been adequately defined, it is the golden key to success.

We hope not only to define the concept of and the reason for positive thinking but also to explore the results of negative thinking. Through research and experiment it was found there are many factors that govern the learning process. These elements are not accounted for in the "stimulus and response" theory that has dominated educators and education for many years.

The results of this research brings out evidence that a student's ability to learn depends on many aspects of mind conditioning. These include everything that the student has seen and heard from the moment he was born, and their effects upon him, the condition of his health, the influence that associations with others has on him, and the methods used in teaching him both at home and in school.

The reader should realize that the mind consists of the conscious and the subconscious. The subconscious mind serves as the storage area for the human computer; **the conscious mind operates the computer and programs the information to the subconscious.**

When the computer works on negative material, the feed-back to the conscious mind, of course, will be only negative; when it receives positive material, the feed-back will be entirely positive.

The cells of the mind carry on chemical activities in a highly organized manner, not randomly. In the transfer of thought from the conscious to the subconscious the electrical energy developed travels in a maze of circuits through synapses (switches), neurons (condensors), and other complicated entities.

Alexander Rich, a professor of biophysics at M.I.T., compared the operation of the human cell in controlling activities on a molecular level with the way in which an electronic computer functions in process control. He stressed at the 1962 Wescon Convention that the computer has a long way to go before it can match the cells of the mind in capabilities. Although today's computer boasts of an "informal density" of 1,000 to 10,000 units per inch, the human brain cell can pack 10 to 100 million information units per inch.

Rich estimated that the human central nervous system contains 10 to 100 billion such cells, each with a storage capacity equal to that of one IBM 7090 computed. If Rich is close to being correct, the human mind has a total storage capacity for all known information in the entire world with room to spare. The mind has many characteristics not found in a computer, such as the ego, desires, *the taste of success,* thinking, reasoning, emotions, etc.

For these reasons, we question the validity of the I.Q. index. We do not agree that this index is, of itself, a true measure of the amount of information stored in the mind of an individual because it does not take into consideration the storage of both negative and positive conditioning, or areas that are blocked and cannot respond to its thoughts.

The consensus is that negative conditioning produces the greatest number of slow learners and those with low

I.Q.s. Blocked areas of the mind are caused by too many conflicting thoughts or statements that dissipate physical and mental energy and prevent the mind from recording and, in many cases, from responding to correct information for the conscious mind.

The research of the contributors to this report shows that when the subconscious mind is reconditioned for positive thinking there is a tremendous increase in both learning ability and I.Q.

It is also the consensus of the contributors that the process of mind conditioning is purely and simply a process of teaching and hypnosis. The mind can quickly receive positive conditioning or reconditioning by means of deep hypnosis. However, it takes a much, much longer time to achieve the same results without deep hypnotic conditioning. The state of hypnosis or the depth of it depend on the degree of concentration and of susceptibility, the amount of conditioning, and the degree of rapture a subject has or shows. Education also depends on these same qualities.

All teachers and educators really are hypnotists and should know how to express themselves; they should understand the results of positive and negative conditioning; they should know a hypnotist only directs or teaches the subject to respond. A susceptible child can be stuck to the floor or to his chair, or he can be blocked so that he remembers nothing that is said, yet he is wide awake or not in a hypnotic state.

The reactions and responses of a student depend to a great extent on the teacher and his selling power. A teacher must always be positive in all of his teachings. To do this, he must be trained to become conscious of what he says and does at all times. He will then be amazed at the changes that take place in his students, will be spellbound with their interest, and will enjoy his role in initiating these great changes.

It is not our teaching system that is at fault, but only

the techniques of the mind conditioning that it employs. Up to this time no one has recognized the fact that negative conditioning can affect the mind so dramatically. Few have consciously conceived of only a positive method of teaching. In recent years biological and biophysical sciences have contributed many new truths to the field of education that have been overlooked. A recent source of such information is a book, "Your Brain, Master Computer" by Margaret O'Hyde.

In view of the research mentioned above, we must conclude that only a positive method of teaching will insure the maximum amount of learning which is the goal that all teachers strive for. This report will give some techniques that will help all teachers to understand how and why they must be positive at all times with their students and in their own thinking.

THE LEARNING BLOCK

1. THE AUTHOR, HIS CONCEPTS OF LEARNING, HISTORY OF RESEARCH

The author of this research report has a major in biology and physical science. His graduate degree is in education. When he was an undergraduate student, he was taught how to hypnotize. The scientific background conditioned him to be inquisitive, with a desire for facts which would explain why for most actions.

His experience and education gave him the chance and desire to do research with mind conditioning. The author's experience covers 15 years district superintendent, 4 years high school principal, 2 years adult principal, and a number of years teaching high school mathematics and science. He was a member of the 35th Infantry Division from Dec. 23, 1940 to June 21st, 1945, during World War II. They fought in the European Theater, and took part in the Normandy, Rhineland, Northern France, Ardennes, and Central Europe battles. He received the following service awards, Bronze Star, Purple Heart, Presidential Citation, five battle stars, and many other minor awards.

During the long service as an educator he continuously searched for means and ways to educate the retarded, and looked for the reasons why retardation took place. His research extends from the kindergarten through all grades. He enlisted help from his staff and associates, such as the school psychologist, teachers, and parents when and wherever he could. He went into research on reading, homework, and mathematics for the retarded.

After the war he took many classes in graduate school, always searching for answers to his questions concerning mind conditioning. Special classes in hypnosis and many meetings with professional hypnotists were held, to consider its values as an educational factor. Meetings with college professors, psychologists, guidance department personnel, and people in many other related fields were held to consider research problems. Help as well as discouragement were received.

The evolution of his educational research took many years. It took him a long time to overcome negative thinking and uncertainty concerning the use of hypnosis with slow learners and low achievers. The work and research with slow learners was slow, until the concept was accepted that hypnosis conditioning was the same as the process used for learning.

This discovery caused him to speculate on the thought process in a different way. It was known that a student's own thoughts and his ability to concentrate were the key to hypnosis and learning. He knew that through hypnosis a slow learner could be conditioned to learn rapidly and easily. The thought therefore struck him: Why wouldn't one's own thoughts be as valuable to him as a teacher's suggestions? If this were true, a process of self-hypnosis would be a big factor in mind conditioning, if a student could be induced to learn to use it. This concept turned out to be a good one, for after a process of self-hypnosis was developed and put to work, most students began to learn with amazing rapidity. The author was amazed to find every student was eager to learn and use the process.

The students who were taught self-hypnosis would practice it every day, then come for deeper hypnosis and guidance once a week. This process was new, therefore; many useful things were learned concerning its use, how to concentrate, what to concentrate on and why.

The process of self-hypnosis was speeded up by telling students when they were under deep hypnosis that they would and could put themselves under easier, and this suggestion worked. Each student was conditioned to self-hypnosis, so that he could relax and reach any level of hypnosis. It was found that it worked best if the students would put themselves into a state resembling a trance but still remain conscious enough to concentrate on the thoughts suggested. They would spend 20 minutes or more a day in this state, concentrating on the things they needed to improve their minds and learning process. There were many items that had to be pointed for each student. Each student had many problems that needed to be solved, each was different from the other, but many or most of their problems were related.

The following are some of the most important thoughts that were used by the students: I am going to enjoy school; I will be able to remember words that I see; I will remember how to spell any word; I will remember the meaning of words that I hear and see; I will be able to read and understand what I read; I am going to see more than one word at a time and know the meanings; I will be able to read without moving my lips; I am going to enjoy reading; I am going to be able to read faster and faster; I am going to be able to concentrate and think deeply; I am going to be able to apply my mind to one subject for long periods of time; I will be able to clear my mind of all interfering thoughts; I will remember everything that I see; that I hear; that I read; my mind is becoming so sensitive that I will be able to learn quickly and easily; all the circuits in my mind are clearing and becoming available for use; all the mental blocks are disappearing and I can think deeply; I am going to feel good; I am going to be happy; I am going to enjoy my home; I am going to have lots of pep and energy; I will recognize negative statements as negative and they will no longer bother me; I can learn anything; etc. The thoughts suggested were adapted to each student and his problems. The student started out with only two thoughts and concentrated over and over on them. He then added a new thought each day and in time began dropping them off the list one by one as his list became longer and longer. Much of the work turned to the subject being taught, such as the multiplication tables, etc. However, many other important problems were also considered, such as: I am going to like my Father; I am going to like my Mother; I will enjoy my home and parents and I will understand them; I am going to do all I can to please them; I want to be liked by everyone.

I repeated to each student over and over, when he was in a deep hypnotic state, most of the items listed above. I kept telling him he could learn, that school was easy, that he would never think that he couldn't learn well; that he would work hard and do his best at all times. The technique of hypnosis and self-hypnosis soon took shape and I found that it works effectively with anyone who can think.

The fact that all of these advantages were realized through the use of hypnosis is not the really important point. It is, instead, that *most of these same results can be accomplished through deep concentration*. It does, however, take longer to achieve the same results and the biggest problem is to condition students to concentrate and think this way about themselves. *However, it can be done.*

The job of mind conditioning is made easier when the parents understand the program and process involved. A good way to start is to give them a copy of a resolution written by Gladys Bevan and titled "A LITANY FOR PARENTS."

"To respect my children and in return
to be worthy of their respect
To praise much and blame little,
To emphasize their success
and minimize their failures
To allow them the dignity of their own personalities,
not trying to make them over to my own desire
To be cheerful and ready to laugh

because children love laughter as they love sunshine
To have infinite patience with my children,
and to make allowances for them
because they have so much to learn
and I myself am not so very wise
To protect my children from my own nerves,
Ill temper, personal prejudices, pessimism, and fears
To help them choose
the life work they are best fitted for,
instead of gratifying through them my personal ambition.
To reserve time and fresh energy for my children
so that I can be their close and interested friend
To fit my children to meet life and people
Bravely, honestly, and independently.
To give my children freedom, but
to teach them to use that freedom sparingly,
So they will not confuse liberty with license.
To show my warm love for my children
as well as conscientiously care for them.
To manage them with intelligence and affection,
and not by condemnation, fear, fault-finding, and nagging.
To guide my children instead of driving them,
to direct their energy instead of repressing it.
To try to understand my children
instead of sitting in judgment on them.
And through all misdemeanors, both trivial and serious,
to love them steadfastly.
May love and understanding help me."

The parents must be told the facts about mind conditioning, told over and over again that their child is intelligent, that he can be conditioned to learn. Explain to them what you can about positive and negative conditioning, then let them ask questions, have them read this book. The extra effort you expend on your students will be amply repaid.

By Edwin Markham

"There is destiny that makes us
brothers
No man goes his way alone.
The good we send into the lives
of others,
Comes back into our own."

Some History About Positive Conditioning of the Mind Within the Classroom

Many years of study and research took place within the classroom before an attempt was made to consolidate the findings and develop a teaching process. Also a great amount of effort was devoted to the individual student both at home and in school before an attempt was made to use the results with an entire class.

Before I started the research to develop a classroom technique of mind conditioning I knew the following: I knew that hypnosis or mind-conditioning in depth worked quickly and easily with the individual student but could not be used per se in the classroom. I had helped a large number of students through depth conditioning with astounding success. I found an elementary classroom teacher using hypnosis to condition her students in the classroom many years before this research was started, in fact it was back in the late 1930's. This teacher did not know what she was doing or why. It was simply a method that had been tried with her when she was a little girl in a private school. She did as so many teachers do, teach as she was taught. Not long ago in the Los Angeles *Times* this same method was described, as, "They are using hypnosis in the classrooms in Italy." This article explained what great success was being achieved in the schools that were using hypnosis. Pictures were shown of students with their heads on their desks sound asleep. The author recognized what was going on and he kept accounts of the great success in the teacher's classroom; he kept quiet about the process but encouraged her in many ways without letting her and the community know what was going on. However, everyone knew that this teacher could help a slow student to become one of the best in the school.

Many years ago another member of our research team also taught and used a variation of the Italian method with great success and later realized why he was successful.

The fact that our research team knew that students could be helped without the deep mind conditioning led it to set up the experimental classroom methods, experimenting first one way and then another, with elementary, junior high, senior high, and some college students.

In their research the contributors to this book worked with as many phases of mind conditioning as they could think of. They delved into positive mind conditioning in the classroom; with a mixture of positive and negative conditioning; then considered negative situations both in the home and at school; and finally tried to condition only one class of students a day with positive methods. They worked for two semesters with the same group but with only one teacher using this technique, then with two teachers, and finally with most of the teachers and the home forming a part of the program.

Throughout all this research, the value of positive mind conditioning stood out so clearly that the students recognized that something good was happening to them. It was superior to any other method that could be devised and produced results far beyond expectation.

The reason for this success is that most slow learners have been conditioned to be "dumb," and are blocked, but are now being reconditioned to learn, i.e., they are being de-hypnotized. They were conditioned to be stupid, to be mean, to be unattentive in class, to no longer care. The circuits of the mind were blocked by fear, guilt, worry, and other negative thoughts; by hearing negative criticism of their ability from parents, friends, other students, and teachers.

Summary

1. Positive mind conditioning works at all levels of intelligence and at all ages.
2. It works when only one teacher is using it and its results carry over to other subjects.
3. Positive conditioning of the mind works better if the teacher continues the conditioning process with the same group for more than one semester.
4. It works even better when more than one teacher uses it.
5. The ideal situation is that in which all teachers of a given group of students cooperate with one another and with the parents.

2. SCIENTIFIC CONCEPTS

Some of the most recent reports by scientists are headed: Scientists launch mass effort to find how human memory works; Scientists seek clues in life-cycle mystery; Scientists have photos which reveal actions of genes in insect cells: Environment impact on personality stressed; Scientists see brain as trigger of disease; Brain, not organs, sees and hear, tests show; Studies show brain's control over hormones; Way opened for new treatment methods as science pinpoints moments of learning; Complexities of cells detailed by scientists; DNA is the master blueprint of life, RNA carries out the instructions of life from the DNA located in the nucleus.

These are only a few of the reports made on recent studies of the mind. All of them were reported in print in the Los Angeles *Times*. Scientists from all over the world are reporting their findings on how the brain functions, how it stores its information and cross-files it in other cells, how DNA and RNA stores information and in turn give out its instructions to all parts of the body and mind, how the great computer is conditioned or programmed to respond. They have explained how negative programming causes sickness and disease. They have found that throughout life, each of us carries an amazing "unwritten diary" tucked away in the brain. Its entries are our experiences —what we saw, heard, touched, smelled, tasted, and thought. Taken together, we call this record of former events—memory. Before you can file a letter, it must be written. And before your brain can "file" an event, it must be experienced.

All of these scientific facts support the author's theory

that intelligence, hate, fear, dislike for school, phobias, etc. are all learned behavior. Therefore: the underlying psyche of such disturbances are conditioned disturbances. The removal, then, of the undesirable behavior is simply the re-programming of the mind; the overcoming of the negative, by programming the positive over and over, until the mind computes the desired results. This will take care of the so called underlying psyche and you will have a lasting change.

The author takes the liberty to enter plates or drawings from his college human anatomy notebook into this book. These were made when he was doing graduate work at U.S.C. The plates illustrate much of the information known to man about the brain and its storage areas. They will help explain and locate some of the terms and ares used in his book.

The plates that show the ribosomes of DNA and RNA are new. DNA and RNA are some of the findings of recent scientific research. Scientists are very busy studying these phenomenon and new reports of their progress are made regularly.

Every school system with its entire staff of teachers must use positive mind conditioning in cooperation with the parents if the system is to educate its students to their ultimate abilities. The teachers must be the directors who guide the student in positive thinking and in abolishing negative thinking in every way possible.

Some Facts About the Mind and Brain That Re-inforce All the Reasons for Positive Mind Conditioning

The cortex of the brain controls all the reflex actions of the body, including those of the muscles, nerves, and organs.

The pituitary gland in the brain is the master gland that regulates the secretion of hormones throughout the

NEURON CELL

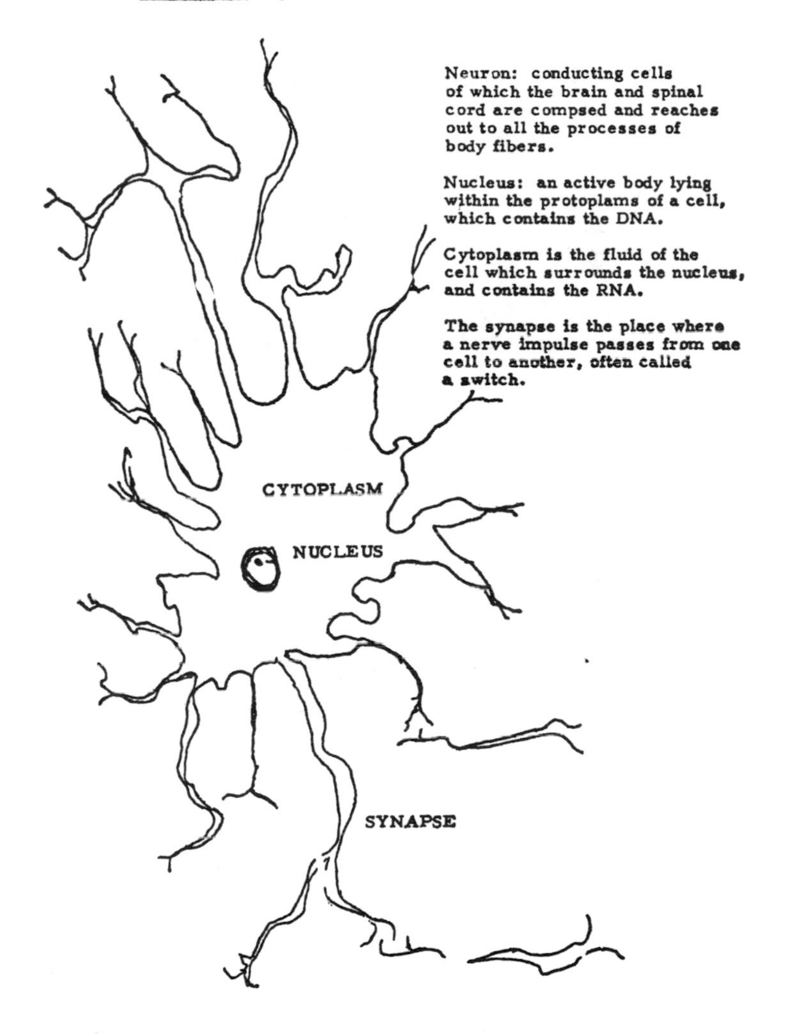

Neuron: conducting cells of which the brain and spinal cord are compsed and reaches out to all the processes of body fibers.

Nucleus: an active body lying within the protoplams of a cell, which contains the DNA.

Cytoplasm is the fluid of the cell which surrounds the nucleus, and contains the RNA.

The synapse is the place where a nerve impulse passes from one cell to another, often called a switch.

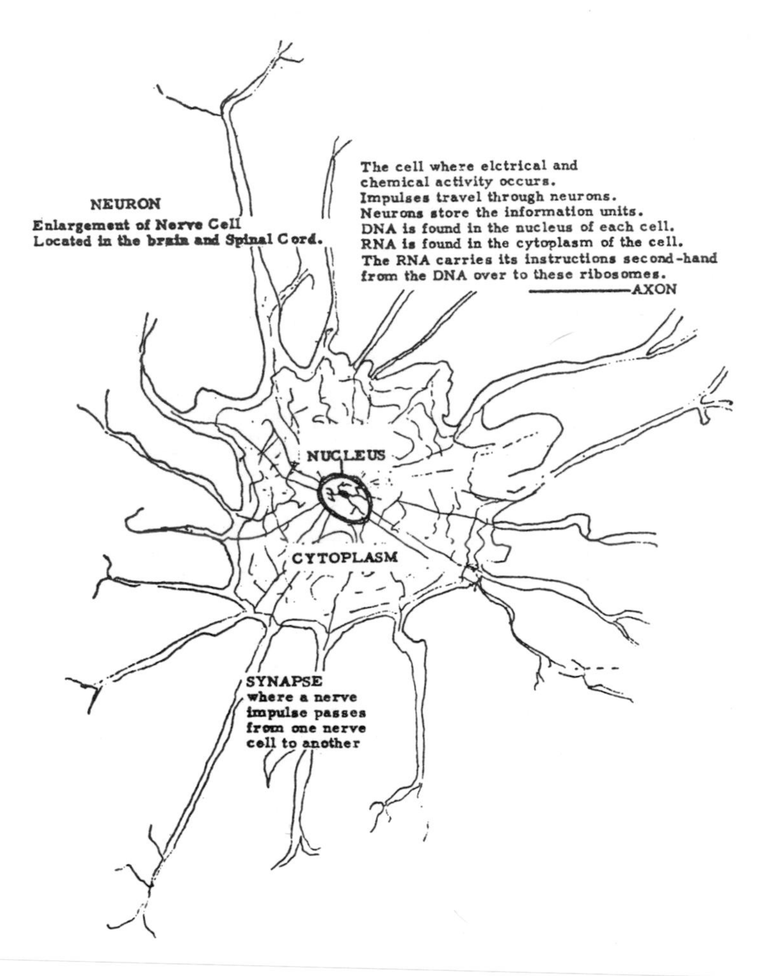

body. The disorders to which it is subject speed up disorders in other parts of the body that are dependent upon the hormone supply.

The thalamus, or midbrain, is the center controlling the subconscious mind. The frontal lobe is thought to be the control center for the conscious mind. It is well known that both the conscious and subconscious draw from the

The DNA records the information and commands the RNA.

The RNA is an exact copy of the DNA.

The RNA carries out the orders of the DNA.

PROTEINS OR ENZYMES

The DNA and RNA have been explained in two ways; they are like a chain, and like a moving picture film. They have been given the name of ribbonsomes, for in each case, they can be stretched out into long ribbons.

DNA + RNA

The DNA and the RNA have ribbons. of protein (enzymes) wrpped around the walls.

There are many kinds of proteins which differ in compound and color.

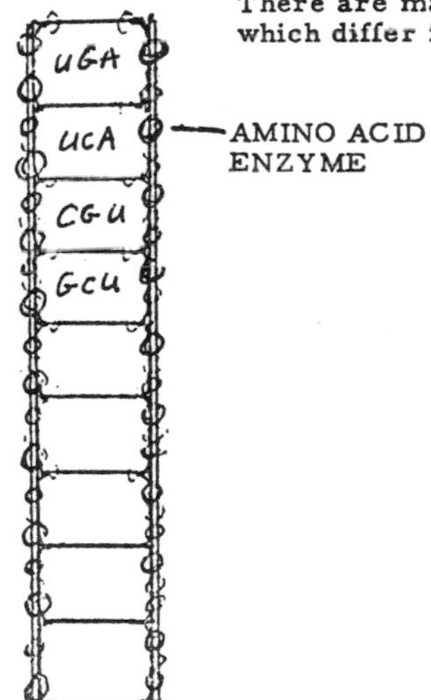

DNA + RNA

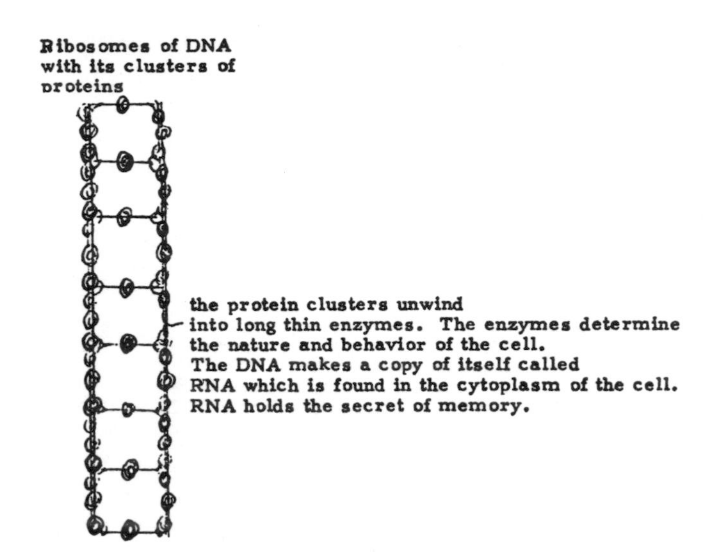

The ribosomes are described to be like a moving picture film or like a chain.

entire brain and affect both each other and the entire brain.

The research that is being carried on at the University of California at Los Angeles on the study of the brain shows that the brain is the trigger mechanism, or cause, of many ailments and diseases. It also shows how the hypothalamus tells the pituitary when to turn on or shut off the flow of the control hormone gonadotropin. There is a chain of command within the brain that is of great importance to the health and behavior of all individuals. It is hoped that by controlling these specific chemicals the health of a person can be improved.

It is common medical knowledge that over fifty percent of those who go to doctors for treatment have complaints that cannot be explained organically. Researchers hope to be able in time to control these complaints by controlling the chemicals in the brain.

The outstanding research on the brain that is being

conducted at M.I.T. in order to build a better computer, shows that the mind is so complex that science will never be able to construct a machine having the capabilities of the human brain. To duplicate just its storage area alone would require a building two miles square and ten miles high.

M.I.T. has recently developed a very fine educational film that illustrates how the computer works and what can be expected of it in the near future. This film, titled the Thinking Machine, covers many aspects that are common to both the mind and the computer. Narrated by John Wayne (the actor) and by Dr. Weisner (scientist) of M.I.T. the film shows how the brain uses electrical signals drawn from its storage area and how the computer reacts in the same fashion. It illustrates how the computer must first be programmed before it can give answers of any kind.

This film explains how when a person is born his mind contains a certain built-in program of rules known as instinct; these rules control or at least have a lot to do with his mental reactions throughout life.

The film gives a very outstanding illustration of perception. It explains how the mind sees only what it has been programmed to see. It also explains two kinds of behavior. It shows how the mind uses both but how a machine can use only rule behavior. The film demonstrates the measurement of the electrical signals in the brain, shows instinctual behavior, how machines learn through perception, and many other interrelationships of mind and machine.

Each and every part of our body responds to some extent to how we think and correlate its functions; as we move our hands, feet, our muscles, they are correlated and respond to the mind. How we think governs how we respond. Our thoughts control our brain and hence much of the response of our body. Therefore, the way in which our mind is conditioned to think determines how we react. Our happiness, skills, personality, and success depend on our habitual reaction.

When we go on to the next step, to mind conditioning, we should think of how we can improve our mental health and of all the means we can take to induce the mind to respond to the process of education, or to what is being programmed into the mind.

There should be no argument as to the ability and capacity of the mind to store information. The storage capacity is there; everything we see and hear is recorded in the mind. Therefore, the real problem is to condition the mind so that it will make this information available to the conscious mind as needed.

The existence of mental blocks is well known. Circuits from the subconscious to the conscious or perhaps circuits from one storage area to others become obstructed. It is very easy to demonstrate how the flow of mental energy in the mind of a susceptible student can become so impeded that he becomes stuck to his chair or forgets his name. We know that these things can happen but we do not clearly understand why they do. We also know that it is impossible to block the mind with positive statements; only negative suggestions can accomplish this.

The brain waves of most students with bad mental blocks are abnormal; when these blocks are removed, these waves return to normal. This indicates that the switches or synapses, of which the mind has billions, have either been opened or closed; it is hard to determine what action does take place but the open-switch theory is more plausible. Some psychologists have in recent years thought that all students who cannot learn well or who have a mental block and abnormal brain waves, have a brain injury. These blocks or open circuits could be considered to be brain injuries, but the causes of these open circuits and the ways and means of overcoming them are the important things to know.

We know that some of these open circuits are caused by negative conditioning; we have also found it impossible to induce them with positive conditioning. Therefore, it is the belief of the research team that they must all be due to negative conditioning if they are induced blocks or injuries.

Research has shown that these blocks will disappear if the student is constantly reconditioned with positive thoughts.

Teachers should strive to control the thoughts of their students by means of positive mind conditioning. This will at times seem an impossible chore since even with deep hynotic conditioning such efforts may seem to be unsuccessful. However, with sufficient conditioning, the mind will begin to respond. Teachers will have to take their students as they are and work at this level to achieve the desired results. We dream of the day when we will have students who are not blocked, students who have not been conditioned negatively, the day when all mental blocks have been eliminated. This happy thought can become a reality but not without the cooperation of all teachers and parents if we are to achieve the ultimate in the education of our students.

It is our firm contention that the gifted can be helped, even if there is no indication of a mental block; they can be shown and trained how to use their minds more thoroughly. However, this is the duty of all teachers to all of their students, regardless of the level of learning and abilities. Although it is hard to imagine a school consisting exclusively of bright, open-minded students, students without blocks, this can be the case and we must strive to make it so.

Research can be found going on in all the Universities but most of it is in related fields. Medical centers are working with the retarded with success. A report in the *Reader's Digest,* January 1965, which was condensed from *Today's Health,* published by the American Medical Association, titled "They Speed Up Slow Minds" tell of the success of Connecticut's Seaside Regional Center for the mentally retarded. This report lists many reasons why Seaside has such wonderful success, it states "what accounts for Seaside's success is not one thing, but a combination of fresh elements. One of the most important is the encouragement of close family relationships. Most institutions for the retarded have strict regulations. Seaside programs are informal. It keeps its door open. It says to parents: Come any time; walk right in; you don't need a pass. Feed your child, dress him. Just say the word and take him home. We're delighted you can do something for him that we can't.

"Another factor in Seaside's success is the unusual amount of personal attention its patients receive. They live, play and go to class in small groups. But Seaside's greatest single contribution to the care of the retarded is its training program for men and women 17 years of age and older who can be taught to be useful workers."

The entire program is built around encouragement, success, love, praise, and keeping the mind and body busy.

Dr. Leonard W. Mayo, Chairman of President Kennedy's 1962 Panel on Mental Retardation states, "The basic principles on which the Seaside program is based are so sound that they should be widely duplicated, and in one way or another they are bound to be." Other states have made a study of its operations, and Colorado and Illinois recently established regional centers of their own.

A trainee from Seaside becomes accustomed to moving around in the community; he is placed in a job outside the center, in time moves away from the home and goes on his own. A Seaside social worker continues to look after him until he can go on his own. These trainees are the caliber of mentally retarded, who in the past were not reached or were incapable of becoming citizens on their own.

According to Dr. Glasky, a biochemist, animals that

had received magnesium pemoline experienced an increase in amount of R N A manufactured in their brains. Untreated animals did not. The implication is not only did the drug stimulate the manufacture of R N A, but proves R N A is the molecule of memory so long sought by researchers.

Science is, in fact, disproving in a number of ways the long-held belief that a person is pretty much stuck with the brain he is born with. Animal experiments showed there are several ways that the individual's inbred behavior pattern can be altered.

Research explained that underprivileged children can be stimulated by exposing them to a variety of experiences involving the senses. It was also revealed that desirable brain changes can be caused even in adult rats who are switched to enriched environments.

According to researchers, the drug used on animals already is undergoing clinical trials on humans at the State University of New York at Albany. If the humans respond as the animals did, they will be able to retain the memory up to 12 times longer and will gain in R N A molecules.

We believe such research is important to our growth in education. We contend that memory can and is developed and through proper stimulation and environments, that R.N.A. molecules are stimulated and show a gain without the use of drugs. We further believe, the human inbred behavior patterns can be changed much easier than those of lower animals. The reasons for this belief are; animals must live their lives mostly from instincts and little from conditioned behavior; human behavior becomes conditioned or learned behavior that overcomes most of the inbred behavior patterns.

Our body is maintained through a highly organized process of chemical actions. The health of the body and mind depend upon a chemical balance. The low voltage electric current needed to send and receive the impulses that control the functions of our body is chemically manufactured. It is well known, most of our ailments are due to a chemical imbalance. These chemical imbalances are caused to a great extent by how we think. Hate, fear, worry, and many other negative processes cause a chemical change to take place.

The mind controls the flow of impulses to our organs and glands, it regulates the secretion of the glands, some almost directly by our thoughts (the secretion of saliva, pancreas, juices, the flow of adrenalin, kidneys, etc.) which in turn can and does change the chemical balance of our bodies. There are many thoughts that trigger chemical imbalances. It is known that when a chemical imbalance is severe enough, learning is impaired. Many things concerning the feeling of well being depend upon a good chemical balance; such as, energy, ego, desire, ability, our senses etc. It also has been discovered that magnesium pemoline will stimulate an increase in the amount of R N A manufactured in the brain, and will aid memory.

Then it is imperative that the research be extended to the power of our mind, how our thoughts control the mind, the amount of control our mind has over its own chemical balance, for it has a relationship that is important for us to know. We are sure, what you think, hear, and see has a relationship to the chemical balance of the mind. How the mind is conditioned and trained to respond plays a big part in the quantity of RNA, memory, and the mental health of the mind.

3. THE TEACHER

When a computer has been programmed with wrong information (the equivalent of negative statements), it must be corrected by repeatedly inserting correct statements or answers into the computer; in this way negative statements are overcome.

This is also the case with the mind. As teachers we must repeat over and over "you are intelligent, you can learn this, this is easy, I like you, let me help you remember that you have a great mind, etc." Remember that we are not turning away from stimulus and response (for this is why stimulus and response worked in the past), but are using it even more in some phases of positive conditioning. We must stimulate desires of the students, we must work on their ego, we must develop a wonderful self-image and keep right on stimulating them to be better.

We must prepare ourselves to condition and program these human computers by having our work planned a few days ahead. We should write down as many positive statements as we can think of for each class. Until it becomes a habit, write down the things not to say. Never say that a subject is hard to learn (don't build up *your* ego this way). Never tell a student that he is dumb, never make etaoin shrdlu etaoin shrdlu etaoin shrdlu etaoin etaoinnn fun of him, never tell a class that no one in it is intelligent enough to earn an A, never tell them how many you plan to fail. We teachers should be above calling our students gangsters, morons, idiots, numbskulls; they may be hearing this constantly at home and from their friends.

Talk about how wonderful the day is, how alive you feel, how wonderful the students look. It is well during the first part of the semester to tell them what they are going to be learning, how interesting and easy it will be. Teach them to concentrate for long periods of time on one subject. Remedial concentration as well as many aspects of the subject matter can be taught through stories. Remember to tell them that how they think is how they are, that if they are sleepy they are thinking it. Tell them to think big, to think well of themselves since if they don't, no one else will. Get them to ask questions and then be sure you are really answering them. Explain, explain, explain!

It has been known for many years that everything a person sees and hears is recorded in his mind, that it is never erased. It is recorded in the form of pictures and sounds and anyone can be made to again experience any event of the past more vividly than it was originally experienced. It is also known that events that one hears or sees are cross-filed in the mind to such an extent that while thinking of one thing, associated events will be recalled.

Recent research on what is known as DNA or the actions of deoxyribonucleic acid the basic substance that controls much of the destiny of all living things, may help to clarify the process of memory and how the mind stores all of its information. Research and practical experience are producing more and more evidence that children who are below normal in intelligence can receive a great deal of benefit from formal schooling in their present condition. However, with a proper mind conditioning program, some can be brought up to normal and many above. Also, intelligence is not one separate score. Most mentally retarded chilren have been conditioned to be slow; they have been blocked. However, they can be reached in a variety of ways. (Don't forget that their minds are recording the same as yours.)

We must constantly keep before us the ultimate needs of these children. We must remember some of these blocks; in fact, most of these blocks can be removed through positive conditioning. Furthermore, we must not forget that the average and the gifted students also have certain mental blocks.

Everyone has mental blocks of one kind or another. Over a period of time everyone receives negative conditioning, for it is everywhere, on radio, and television, in our homes, and churches, and with our companions. The most intelligent student has had the advantage of more positive conditioning than the others. Many understand to a degree negative statements when they hear them but are not affected to the same extent as the susceptible or slow students. Our research has proven that most of the slow students are very susceptible; hence they *may potentially be the most intelligent of all,* if these blocks can be eliminated.

We must be continually trying to push these children as far as they can go up the ladder of success. The greatest failing of most teachers today is their inability or unwillingness to make a realistic aprpaisal of the child's present abilities and then begin to teach him at this level.

We have thousands of students who are convinced that they are "stupid." Every teacher has heard students say to them, "I am too dumb to learn that," or "I can't do that," etc. These students are sure that it is useless to study, or even to try to learn since it will do them no good. Many of them will inform their teachers at the end of the semester that they are stupid or dumb and can't learn very well. They will also say that they hate the subject, they hate the school, they hate their home.

These students are blocked; their mental image of themselves is at a very low ebb. They are unhappy, dejected, and miserable.

I have found that the damage to the mind from "blocks" can be repaired by reconditioning the mind through hypnosis. Past mistakes, failures, and negative experiences which inhibit the learning process can be forgotten or reduced to little importance. New desires (or motivation) can be developed and once this takes place, the student becomes happy, confident and creative; he knows he can learn anything as quickly as anyone else. Some of these students are so happy that they now can learn that they state: "I am now a brain, I am going to be a brain, I can learn quickly now, I love school," etc. Their comments vary, but their report cards indicate they are now indeed scholars, not just students. They are happy, not dejected, and are willing to tell anyone at once that they can learn anything. They have a wonderful image of themselves and a relaxed personality.

Teachers have not been told how to recondition the mind or why it should be reconditioned. In many cases, they add to the present mental blocks by doing the very things that caused these blocks originally. That is, they assign work beyond the ability of the student, they scold, lecture, and demand the impossible of him.

The mind differs from a computer in many ways; it is more complex, it has an ego and many desires. It likes the taste of success, it thinks, reasons, and worries.

A child worries more than we think he does. What he worries about is mostly negative and one negative thought brings on another. That is why we as teachers must continually tell and show them how much easier learning can be, keep as much worry from them as we can, build up their ego, develop their desires, give them a taste of success, see to it they are successful in much of their work. Be sincere but be unrelenting in your desire for them to succeed. You must repeatedly explain that they are intelligent, that they can learn this subject, and need to know it. Say it as many times and in as many ways as you can think of saying it. This book will say this over and over in many ways since we are conditioning teachers to condition students on a positive basis; to do so, you must be convinced.

Develop their ability to visualize and to use their imagination. Experiments show that a student can improve his comprehension 100% by consciously using two techniques; these are visualizing details, re-reading a second time to select the important facts. It has been proven that visualization improves all skills, even in sports. Games are replayed in the mind of an athlete; a game is played in his mind before it takes place. He sees himself doing the things that he will have to do well if he is to succeed in the game. Therefore, have the student read the problem, visualize it, and then reread it. Teachers should remember the concept that I.Q.s never change have been struck down in many directions. The advocacy of these concepts have lost votes, because many of their so called morons have gone on to college, obtained Ph.D. degrees and became great in their field. Many others became great in their field without a formal education.

There was a time when most students were told not to go on to college, if their I.Q. was low. Colleges gave examinations and advised students to go home, if their results were below the school norm. There was no place in the colleges for students unless they were above average.

Today students are given a chance, they may enter Junior Colleges and make up their deficiencies. Quite a number of students who have low I.Q.s and are dropouts, become good students at the college level and graduate from college. Success stories concerning low I.Q. students may be found almost everywhere one looks.

Some of these success stories told by the author are as follows. He tells one of a very prominent man, who has held many high positions in education, such as state superintendent, district superintendent, president of a state college from which he graduated, along with a top position as an educator in Washington, D.C., who was told when he went to college to go home. He was told his I.Q. was 72 and he could not be successful in college and should not waste the money or time going to college. However, he graduated with honors. He later received a Ph.D. degree and went on to become a great man in his field.

When he returned to the State College as president, he looked up his records and found his I.Q. recorded as 72 or, as he puts it, a moron.

One of the author's famous stories concerns a boy from one of his schools in the midwest, who tested over and over to have an I.Q. of 74. This boy was short English credits when it came time for him to graduate from high school. He was sure that he would not return to school and make up the short credits and was just as sure he would never wish to go on to college. Therefore this student was given enough credits to graduate. The student wanted to farm. He had a dislike for school. His parents gave him a farm when he graduated from high school. He moved to the farm and farmed it for two years and then something happened. He and his parents came to school and announced that he was going to the State University.

His credits were sent into the University and he registered for the Fall term. Afterward he was told not to go and why. When the first semester ended, it found him with four D's and one fail. The University called him in and explained the point system and told him he had a very low I.Q. and should drop out at the end of the first semester. At the end of the second semester he was called in again, for his second semester's grades were four Cs and one D, and told he should drop from school. However, they did tell him they could not and would not kick him out of school.

He registered for the next fall in the spring and spent the summer studying. He earned all B's the third semester and mostly all A's for the rest of his college years, also obtained a Ph.D. degree.

This is one of the cases that caused the author to take a better look at his belief concerning I.Q.s and what he should tell the students who were graduating from high school. He has asked himself many times, how many of my students stayed away from school, because I told them they could not be successful in college? Who am I to tell them not to go on to school?

Dr. John Sexton (ex-superintendent of the Pasadena school system) used to tell a story concerning two boys who were voted by the faculty of his school system to be the greatest failures. These boys became national figures in their fields. They were millionaires. They had done more for science and the furtherance of our society than any other two students to graduate from his school system. He told many other stories concerning students with genius ability, who were failures in life and ended up on skid row.

Dr. Sexton contended over and over that I.Q.s have very little to do with predicting success. They measure only knowledge at the moment. They do not measure interest or ability to grow when the right inspiration takes place.

4. TEACHING MACHINES

Why the teaching machines? Can they really teach? What is their potential? What must teachers do to meet their challenge? These and many, many other questions must be asked and answered within the next few years.

During the school year 1962-63 over one million children were exposed to the technique of learning by means of machines and programmed information. Through research, it has been proven that children can learn the facts of a subject in a very few hours, facts that would take an average class an entire semester or even a year to learn. These students were not the pick of the crop: they did not have a high I.Q. but were average and, in many cases, even very slow. The teaching machines, greatly benefiting the retarded and the slow students, are doing what has been considered to be impossible.

Teaching machines are being enthusiastically adopted by educators and psychologists; it is expected that programmed instruction will soon eliminate some of the teachers. Universities throughout the nation, all the way from Stanford to Harvard, are reporting on the results of experiments with programmed instruction. It is not at all improbable that machines may take over a great part of the teaching program and be very successful. Why machines?

The reason why teaching machines can do just what it is claimed they can do is very simple. They work with the individual child. There is no tension or pressure. The *machine is positive in its teaching;* it leaves no room for failure. Every student must be able to do the work, since facts and answers are given almost simultaneously. Students do not have to wait days for an answer and perhaps never receive it. The lessons are prepared ahead of time, in a concise form, with the questions taken directly from the program. These questions are asked and answered at the same sitting. Students do not return home with stacks of homework that they do not understand; instead they have proper directions at all times. The machine has no negative thoughts in its programs. It does not allow the student time to daydream, to harbor negative thoughts and resist authority. If the machine is not successful, it is blamed instead of the student. The subject was not programmed to the advantage of the student or as well as it might have been.

No one shouts, belittles, lectures, or builds up an emotional situation, in which the mind becomes twisted with hate, fear and resentment toward the teacher, authority, and the subject matter. There are no deadlines to meet and no failing grades are sent home.

Educators are now busy writing new books and developing new courses of study, so that when a subject is taught, the student will know not only the facts but why they are true. New methods of teaching mathematics will clearly show why we factor and how this is done. The student will be expected to do the reasoning behind all of these facts and laws in the new mathematics. Instead of being speeded up, the teaching of mathematics will be slowed down; it will take time for the student to do the reasoning and discovery unless these become a *programmed process.*

There is a good reason why this trend to teaching machines is taking place. The colleges and universities are complaining that the students of mathematics and science know the facts and laws but cannot reason about them because they do not know how and why these laws came about; they just know the laws. Their complaint is that the students are unable to form new and imaginative ideas.

If teachers are to direct the mind conditioning of the students to enable them to learn through discovery and still cover the same amount of material as before, teachers will have to use the programming and perhaps the machines along with classroom instruction.

Now that we have covered what teaching machines do for the student and why they are so successful, it will take but little imagination to see why classroom teachers must abandon the traditional methods for positive conditioning, and why we have been so repetitious; *one must be positive.*

Teachers can meet the challenge of programmed and machine teaching by using positive mind conditioning, and doing it so well that there will be no doubt as to its value in the classroom. (Remember the resistance to audio-visual aids.) They can give the child many things that a machine cannot give them. They can prepare their programs for the minds (computers) that they have in their classrooms with greater success, and develop these computers to respond through discovery. They can teach them to be constructive, to visualize, to concentrate, and to reflect their talents in all directions. *It is the program that teaches, not the machine.* The machine is only a gadget that holds the material and allows the child to work by himself. The teacher can keep his class from having tedious work, as it is characteristic of machine teaching and of most of our present classes; he can make the class become alive with lots of enthusiasm and enrich the pupils with knowledge that a machine could not possibly give. The students will learn how to imagine themselves successful; they will not need a box to hold the information for them since they will find success.

5. AUDIO-VISUAL AIDS

Audio-visual aids are tools for positive education. That is why they have played such an important role in education for so long. When they are used properly, the work is explained before the films, pictures or field trips take place and it is then explained again afterwards. This approach helps to instill the information in the mind, helps in cross-filing it in the mind, and insures that it is clearly recorded. The importance of perception in learning and of visualization as a tool in learning is only imperfectly recognized in our educational process. Students can be taught to visualize, to the extent of reseeing entire pages in a book. The power of perception helps to control their thinking. Students are not born with pictures in their minds. These come from the mind conditioning they receive. Some students have been taught visualization so well that they have photographic minds; they can recall and resee what they have stored up in their minds.

The process of visualization can be taught to all students. Everyone at times recalls pictures of what he sees. This is done by practice; one looks at a picture and then looks away and resees it. Closing one's eyes and recalling something that has just happened is another kind of visualization. This is a process of concentration that disciplines the mind. Students find this process easy since it is almost akin to the daydreaming that they can do so well. Change this daydreaming to visualization of the subject matter, of the pictures you show, and of the field trips taken.

The process of visualization should be a "must" for all, be they gifted, average, or even very slow. If visualization can be achieved by a few, it can be achieved by all. Replace their daydreams with really interesting things to visualize. This process can be made a part of reading, of story telling, of mathematics—in fact, of all activities including sports. Ben Hogan mentally played each shot before he made it; many golfers have developed their powers of visualization to help them play a better game.

Scientists have found that it is now possible to tell by means of instrumentation the exact moment that learning becomes fixed, or set, in the brain as new knowledge. Audio-visual aids help to achieve this faster than any other means.

In recent scientific experiments with the mind in many of our large universities, it was found it is the brain, not the organs, that sees and hears. All of the test results prove this to be true. Through electrical stimulation of certain areas in a patient's brain, images and sounds have been produced. Some of these came from things the patient had seen and heard in the past; others were thought to be hallucinations. This situation is encountered frequently when a patient is fully conscious during brain surgery. The sounds and images are very vivid.

Deep concentration is a process of conditioning that is the first real key to learning. The process of visualization is almost as important. Deep concentration means that the mind is attuned to only one thing. At times, it will have mental pictures of what it is doing and all other thoughts have been banished. Such concentration is most effective when all tension and fear have been released. This is when learning or mind set is recorded, when knowledge becomes fixed in the brain. Positive mind conditioning is essential if we are to achieve the best possible results in our teaching.

All teachers should employ audio-visual aids as often as they can find and devise good material to show. They should use the blackboards, the bulletin boards and all other devices that can help to picture the lesson for the day.

A good audio-visual aid is to talk about what the students are doing, making copies of the work, labeling and explaining each part. Have them visualize the work after the drawings, pictures, etc. have been removed, and at times re-emphasize the main points by replacing the audio-visual material, re-running it, etc. This helps set the information firmly in the mind.

This technique should be used at all levels, in all grades; it is a most important tool for helping the retarded. Teachers should keep themselves informed regarding such teaching aids as field trips, exhibits, motion pictures, demonstrations, graphs, charts, maps, diagrams, etc. They should check with the schools, agencies, and industries within their comunity.

Art can play a vital part in teaching by means of visual aids. Positive mind conditioning and art give the teacher and student a wonderful chance to do many things which are very closely related to the visual and perceiving program. The following suggestions have proven to be very effective for this purpose.

1. The classroom should be pleasant and contain suitable bulletin boards and other visual aids.

2. The art class should teach ways and means of developing pleasant surroundings in the home and in school.

3. The art class should give instruction on the values of perceiving and on the use of art as valuable means of learning and expression.

4. Art classes should study some of the great works of art and be helped to discover why these works are great.

5. Students who seem to enjoy art and who are adept at it should be encouraged to continue their study beyond the appreciation stage by taking more advanced classes.

6. All classes should make every effort to show how their subject and art are correlated.

7. The apperception of students seems to be best expressed through art and if taught properly will help assimilate their ideas.

8. Art students should be trained to see and to know what they see.

6. MOTIVATION

A student learns best when he has been motivated to do so. Past success and a reasonable basis for expecting future success are the greatest factors in motivation. On the other hand, nothing destroys motivation as quickly as punishment or annoying consequences. Nothing blocks the mind, the desires, and the ego faster and tends to discourage further efforts to learn. We must therefore avoid demoralizing the pupil and even go to extremes to remotivate him if he has lost his incentive. We must sometimes temporarily drop the subject being taught in order to avoid annoying or punishing the pupil or in any way sabotaging the motivation we have helped him to acquire.

We should become aware of what negative conditioning is; we should list and clearly define what the student considers annoyances and punishments. We should find ways to eliminate them from our everyday class routine.

A common habit of teachers is to give students poor grades during the first half of a semester in order to get them to work harder. Some teachers like to keep the grade points a secret; this is a practice, that in most cases, only confirms the students in their belief that they are indeed stupid.

Remember that nothing succeeds like success. It is also true that nothing destroys confidence as fast as repeated failure. We are not asking you to give higher grades than those warranted (even though we believe that at times this would help); we ask only that you be fair to the student. It is a good practice to keep the grades in a notebook on top of your desk; make this book available to the students to check their own grades. Show them how you average the grades so that they can keep a running account of where they stand.

Start your teaching at the level of development the pupils have already reached, not above this level. See to it they have some success in the subject being taught, and never cover more matter than they can absorb in the time allotted. Be fair; don't grade the pupil on the basis of misdemeanors. Maybe you yourself were the cause of his misconduct.

A high percentage of teachers put far too much value on final exams. They tend to base the questions in these exams on what they should have covered or on what they think they should have covered, not on what they really did cover. I have known of students who had a B average all semester and who then did not pass the course because they failed in the final exams.

Get your values straight, and keep them straight. This leads to success after success, to good motivation. Students talk more about the unfairness of teachers than about any other deficiency and this unfairness makes them rebel in the classroom. Outline the subject you are teaching so that the students will know what they are to cover during the week, the month, the quarter, and, at times, the semester. Show them as you go along what they are learning; convince them that they have learned something of importance.

As far as possible build your presentation of the subject around things they are interested in. Whet their interest in the subject you are teaching by using audio-visual aids of all kinds, by taking field trips, and by applying antidotes to their negative way of thinking. The importance of perception in learning as a means of motivation is a point every teacher should remember.

Teachers must be interested in the problems of their students. They must try helping them solve their problems and do all they can to gain their confidence.

Good motivation leads to mind *set* or the act of setting

the mind. To obtain a mind set, everything that can be done to prepare them to learn the subject matter for the day must be done.

The best kind of teaching involves an exchange of ideas between the teacher and his students; it helps if he is a good lecturer, but it is essential that he come down to earth to the students' level and answer their questions satisfactorily. When a student leaves a classroom asking more questions than he did when he came in, he is learning and you can be sure that he wants to continue to learn. It's far more important for the student to be able to interpret what you tell him than to parrot it.

7. THE MIND AND HOW WE LEARN

The nature of learning has been studied by scientists, psychologists, and educators for many years and all agree that there are many points that can explain various types of conduct. These include growth, environment, reproduction, curiosity, heredity, confidence, sight, hearing, smell, touch, and many others which are all often grouped under the term "individual differences." The individual differences of human beings are recognized by everyone who deals with learning, and no one questions the fact that these differences have a bearing on the learning process and on diversity of behavior.

There are many definitions of learning; the broadest is that when it takes place an altered mental condition is the result. It is essential to look at the problems of learning from every angle to obtain a broad perspective. There are times when we must use *practical* wisdom, in carefully reappraising the problems of education, and then apply the methods of teaching that works best. Since there is always a reason for all progress in education, we should always be looking for this reason.

If we are to be practical, the following are some of the things that we as educators and teachers should carefully consider:

1. Both positive and negative statements help to condition the mind.

2. Teaching is a process of mind conditioning (or hypnosis).

3. Hypnotic statements are encountered everywhere; in the home, at school, in church; wherever speech is used.

4. Mental blocks are induced by someone close to the subject.

5. Almost every normal child suffers from a mental block of some type.

6. Emotionally disturbed people have been conditioned to be so.

This list would become tiresome if we listed all of the points that we should remember. However, the fact that education and hypnosis or the process of mind conditioning both are the same is one that must be firmly grasped by educators.

There are many degrees in the hypnotic state ranging all the way from a very light to a very deep sleep; the latter is known as a trance or as a state of anesthesia. The hypnotic effect can be so slight that no evidence of it is noticeable; yet it often happens that pain ceases, the subject becomes relaxed or responds to a suggestion. The mind has definitely been altered; this change may be temporary or through conditioning it may become permanent.

Hypnosis is induced in three different ways: by suggestion, by the tiring of one's senses, and by one's own efforts. In most cases, hypnosis is induced by positive statements thatt he subject will realize as facts. The gadgets and equipment used by some hypnotists are only show or they may have some psychological effect. The basic cause of hypnosis is the combination of positive statements made by the hypnotist and the subject's reaction to them.

Through his own thoughts a person can hypnotize himself. He can induce in himself any state or level of hypnosis. His success depends on his ability to concentrate, his susceptibility, and the amount of practice or conditioning he has had. Anyone can be trained or conditioned to enter a state of amnesia.

I have conditioned many students to put themselves into any state of hypnosis; the susceptible ones can be conditioned to enter a state of amnesia in a matter of minutes. Students who are not readily susceptible can be conditioned to self-hypnosis.

Through self-hypnosis, a student learns to concentrate more deeply; it gives him the key to concentration, it teaches him how to clear his mind of all other thoughts and how to keep his mind on one problem for long periods of time.

I wish to point out again that anyone can put himself into a state of hypnosis through concentration; for this reason many students and adults are in a state of hypnosis most of the time. Through their thoughts they have conditioned themselves to be sick, dumb, sleepy, tired, to hate, and to block out anything they do not wish to hear or see. The reasons for attitudes and actions can be traced to the home, the school, and the community. Most of the emotionally ill have through conditioning made themselves ill. Their illnesses are real, even though they have been induced through self-hypnosis. Through self-hypnosis, a person can take away or induce pain, can speed up the flow of blood or slow it down, and can drastically affect many other physical processes.

Then through worry, fear, etc., these things can be and are induced. The same process exists in the mind, for when things are happening and are caused to happen, the nerve circuits are being blocked in the mind to cause them to happen in the body.

A student then who can concentrate deeply enough on one thing can condition himself to be ill, stupid, temporarily deaf or sightless; he can block out his teacher or parents and prevent his mind from computing for him. When these blocks are repeatedly induced, they become permanent unless they are eliminated through some special procss such as positive conditioning of the mind or deep hypnosis.

The conditioning of the mind that takes place in our schools must be so organized that there will be no reasons for mental blocks. We must give the students proper training and proper things to think about. We must get them to understand themselves, their mind and how it functions, and then keep them so occupied with important facts that they cannot help but learn.

A large percentage of people can be hypnotized if someone merely talks to them, or they can hypnotize themselves by concentrating in a certain way. The success of an attempt to hypnotize a person by talking to him depends to a great extent on the faith the subject has in the operator, his ability to concentrate, and the amount of conditioning to which he has been exposed. (These factors also influence the success of education or mind conditioning.) Anyone can induce hypnosis in another through ordinary conversation.

Education and hypnosis are one and the same. Both are processes of conditioning the mind, of altering it. Both processes must convince the subject of their merits before a positive conditioning can take place.

I wish to emphasize again that conditioning is best effected by the use of pictures, models, or the object itself. This approach teaches visualization, convinces the mind, closes the switches of the nervous system for ready learning or conditioning. Deep concentration is a process of conditioning and it is the first real key of learning. Visualization is a part of deep concentration; when both occur at the same time the mind is altered.

One factor in the learning process about which we know very little is the subconscious mind. We know that if we give our subconscious mind a problem, through deep concentration it will come up with the essentials or facts; it works best when the conscious mind is at rest or relaxed. Therefore, we should set aside periods in which definite assignments can be fed to the subconscious. This is accomplished best through self-hypnosis, through the process of concentrating on the essentials, while we are in a state of deep relaxation. Tension and fear slow down the conditioning process of learning and in time will gravely affect the mental health of our citizens.

It is our belief that the full truth about education, the conditioning of the mind, the development and modification of the tendencies that govern the psychological functions, or whatever definition one cares to attach to learning, has never been reached and that it never will be until education is approached on a positive basis.

Shortly after the turn of the century an outstanding psychologist, Dr. C. D. Larson, was very successful in his work with mind conditioning. Dr. Larson wrote an excellent book on his findings, which is titled *THE SCIENTIFIC TRAINING OF CHILDREN,* and which brings out the same facts that are expressed in the present book. Dr. Larson wrote: "It is the truth and a most important truth that a genius does exist in the subconscious of every mind. Every child is born with that interior something which, when developed, can produce remarkable ability, extraordinary talent, and rare genius. It is therefore of the highest importance that the mind be so trained that all of its latent power and capacity be developed, because everybody should be given the opportunity to reach his potential. I believe the dull child has the talent of the bright child and his mind can be made active. It is only a matter of knowing how. I also believe a dull child is dull due to improper conditioning of the mind from childhood. Improper conditioning of the mind could mean that the mind was neglected, that his talents died from neglect and full use of the elements were not brought forth, or he was suppressed, frequently punished without reason, constantly told in many ways that he is dumb; thus his energy drained to the point of following primitive tendencies.

"I believe to suppress energy is not only to waste energy, it is worse than that, for continued suppression will after a while decrease the amount of energy generated.

The less energy one generates in his system, the less he can accomplish.

"Every phase of the environment will produce an impression upon the mind; every impression made upon the mind will count. Therefore, in conditioning the mind we must impress upon it everything that we wish to see developed. We need not hesitate in producing too many impressions as long as the mind is interested, for there is no danger of cramming the mind. The mind is highly sensitive to every impression that enters consciousness; therefore, keep out ridicule and discouragement, for what is impressed upon the mind usually continues all through life, unless removed later on by some special method."

Dr. Larson was born about 50 years too soon. His teachings and writings went unheeded, for he lived at a time when psychology was uncertain in its own field. Educators at this time were not paying attention to psychologists and their ideas. Dr. Larson did not have the advantages of modern science or the facts about the mind that we have today, but he recognized some of the basic truths concerning the mind. He understood how and why so many students were blocked; he knew motivation involved the influence, the effects, and the outcome of an activity and the desire to repeat the activity. He knew that if a person has a satisfactory outcome, it will encourage repetition of the act and that punishment or annoying consequences will tend to discourage the repetition of it and will tend to block the reflexes.

The mind is conditioned through pictures and statements (both positive and negative) but it is also conditioned and altered by its own thoughts. The more a mind hears or thinks in a certain way, the more that mind will react to the type of conditioning it undergoes. Therefore, we must cause the students to think of themselves as being intelligent and capable of learning anything. We must tell them over and over many positive things if we are going to overcome the negative statements they have heard and the negative thoughts they have been concentrating so hard upon.

What should you tell your students? You should tell them over and over that they are intelligent and about their many abilities. Tell them that there is no difference between their ability and that of the best student in the world (except for how they have been conditioned to think). Explain to them that their abilities can be stifled and held back either through negative statements made to them or by their own negative thoughts.

Explain to them that everything they see and hear is recorded upon their mind (as pictures and sound) and how much of it will be cross-filed in their minds and give them the ability to recall the event, depends on how deeply they concentrate. Explain how negative statements or negative thinking block the nerve circuits so that the information stored up in their minds cannot be recalled to their conscious mind.

Remind them often that they can learn to like anything if they will only concentrate on the fact that they like it. Also, keep telling them that to think that they dislike something is negative and that one negative thought leads to another. Therefore, they should never think negatively and cause mental blocks. Explain what negative things are and have the students list negative statements they have heard and negative thoughts they have concentrated on.

A good example to use at this point is their thoughts about food, how their likes and dislikes depend upon how they have been conditioned to think of them. Have them think of a food that they at one time disliked but now like. Ask them why they think their taste has changed. This is a good occasion to insist that how they think is how they are, that how they think is how they have been conditioned to think. Explain to them that they can cause their minds to become sensitive, that they can learn to concentrate, or that they can block their minds to anything. Describe the importance of positive thinking to their future.

Tell them that happiness is a state of mind, that they can be happy or wretched, that it all depends upon how they think. Explain that there are thousands of people who have every reason to be happy but are miserable and unhappy instead. Keep telling them to think about happiness over and over, to think that they are happy, that they love their parents, that they like their home and friends, that they like school and enjoy learning new things, that they want to have a wonderful and powerful mind and to utilize all of their talents. Explain that happiness is an art, that it can be developed or induced. Remind them that happiness is the most important phase of life, that if they are not happy they are the cause of their unhappiness. Keep going over the fact that if they are not learning easily and well, either they have been blocked by someone or they have caused it to happen. Keep telling them that they must help themselves by understanding and discounting negative statements and thoughts and learn to think properly.

Have the students list the things they would like to do and be and then use it as a check list that they often look at and modify as they grow older. Have them set up a plan for the future. The homeroom is a wonderful place to develop such a plan. The list should include such items as the following:

1. I am going to make something of myself.
2. I am going to think of happiness.
3. I am going to learn every new thing that I can while I have the chance.
4. I am going to condition my mind to be very sensitive and receptive.
5. I am going to understand negative statements.
6. I am going to respect myself.

7. I am going to enjoy my home and community.

8. I am going to learn how to study and then study hard.

9. I am going to think well of myself.

The students will help you make this list, they will become very interested in doing so, and they will volunteer things that they know are wrong with their own thinking.

8. CREATIVE THINKING

The mind is a computer; it stores information and cross files it from one storage cell area to another. When the subconscious or computer is properly conditioned, it reacts like a machine. It will answer questions, it will produce stored information, and at times it will bring out related facts.

The mind can reason, it can visualize, it can think. Sometimes it may suggest more than one answer, but at least it can bring out new ideas and often does so. Since the mind can use the information that is stored within it, it can put facts together, compare them, and generate new material. This process is called creative thinking. A creative thinker allows his mind to solve his problems. He frees himself of his own ideas and views and allows the subconscious to compute new ideas, to combine long forgotten facts and experiences with these new ideas. However, in most cases, there must be a problem involved before this process takes place. Artists are creative in art, mathematicians are creative in mathematics or its related field, but seldom is anyone creative outside of his field.

To be creative, the mind must be relaxed and free of other problems so that it can gather its known facts and experiences together and then come up with new ideas or solutions to the problem at hand.

Many of our great inventors, such as Thomas Edison, have said: "I am not sure where the answers come from; I would consciously think over all of my ideas to the problem before I would go to sleep at night. I would relax and sleep on it, and then find the answers ready for me in the morning." Edison also said that "at times the answers would take longer to be computed and would come to me days or weeks later." Such men were creative, they allowed their subconscious to compute the facts and experiences while they slept, and they would expect an answer. *They would recognize that it was the answer* to the problem. This action took place when the problem was too difficult to be computed at once. The computing took place while the conscious mind was at rest, relaxed, and when the men did not allow their own thoughts to interfere. These men learned how to use their minds; they found out that their mind could compute for them and learned when and how to put it to work for them when they had a really difficult problem and could not solve it consciously.

Other great men who were creative thinkers would isolate themselves from all interference; they would be alone with their thoughts. They would then turn their minds loose on the problem, keep notes on their thoughts, and at times would be rewarded with a number of new ideas.

There are other creative thinkers who thrive upon asking questions, reading and studying facts, participating in activities in related fields where they can see, inspect, and probe their problem. These men allow their minds to run at random; they think only of the problem at hand and relate it to what they see and hear. Noise and activity have no adverse effects on their thinking. They can put together and compute new ideas that work but their minds are constantly focused only on the problem.

It has been said quite often that creative thinking cannot be developed, that it is a gift. I feel, on the contrary, that it can be developed. One can develop creative thinking by first grasping the functions of the mind, by understanding how to use ideas, by recognizing new ideas when they are computed and by then putting them to work in solving a problem. These are the chief abilities needed. Creative thinking can be developed, since these things can be taught. The student should be taught to relax, to concentrate on all known facts and possibilities, to clear his mind of all interference, and then let it compute the answers and ideas. He should keep an account of the thoughts that come to him about the problem at hand. He should look for new ideas and then check on them.

It is my belief that the minds of people compute many ideas but that they are not trained to recognize these ideas or prepared to put them to use.

A child does more creative thinking than an adult; his questions and answers indicate this. The thinking of adults becomes so stereotyped that their minds have no energy for creative thinking. Much of his ability for creative thinking is taken away from a child when he goes to school. His mind is occupied with new thoughts, with facts, and his imagination begins to wither. We do not believe small children should be conditioned to be creative or to imagine new things because their minds must first be conditioned to facts. They must learn how to solve problems before they can think creatively about something that is useful. However, from their junior year in high school they should be told and conditioned to think creatively. A junior high school student has enough facts stored in his mind to compute new ideas and he should understand how his mind works.

Creative thinking can be applied to many subjects, such as mathematics, science, art and many others. Our mind is not inactive during sleep; it can compute impressions received during the day. This activity, called by some "dream solutions,' 'is really that of a computer that is never turned off.

Fortunately, we know that all ideas come from suggestion, and hence *can be removed by suggestion.* We also know that students are creative even when they form mental blocks, when they develop an inferiority complex, when they go to sleep full of fear, hate, and unhappiness.

Lead them into a better view of themselves. Teach

them to use both sides of their minds. Teach your students to become aware of themselves and of their abilities. Show them that an open relaxed mind is ready to respond to suggestions, ideas, etc.

Teachers must learn how to program their subjects, how to suggest ideas, how to induce interest, how to obtain a relaxed class, how to visualize a good teaching experience, and be creative with their teaching. Teachers must become aware of their abilities to teach.

9. MIND CONTROL THROUGH BRAINWASHING

It is well known that brainwashing, the dominating of the mind and its thoughts, is being used more and more throughout the world. The effectiveness of this technique depends on a number of factors, such as the susceptibility of the mind, its endurance, and whether the one subjected to it is segregated or separated from his normal way of life. Brainwashing is not new; we are only giving it a new name and explaining how it works.

A susceptible person can be brainwashed without physical abuse by being constantly indoctrinated with half-truths that gradually change to complete falsehoods.

The Nazis proved that after 70 days of wretched food, little sleep, poor quarters, abuse, denial, and defamation, a man's endurance cracks and that any *sudden and unexpected* threat or suggestions puts him in a state of shock. He then obeys unquestioningly and abandons his former loyalties and beliefs. His mind becomes permanently altered by an emotion so strong that it blocks out much of its previous conditioning.

The Russians and Chinese have both proven to the world that there is an art to conditioning the mind. They have used two techniques. One is to keep the mind busy and occupied, the other is to overcome the endurance of both mind and body by physical and psychological abuse.

The Russians have also proved that children taken from their parents when they are three months old and raised in state boarding schools show a very low rate of retardation. The home and community have little chance to affect their mental conditioning. In these boarding schools their minds are conditioned on a positive basis, kept constantly occupied, and given no time to become disturbed or blocked. They are given no opportunity to think negatively about themselves or to hear negative suggestions.

Brainwashing or mind conditioning is practiced throughout the world in all fields. That it is used in psycho-political situations, in salesmanship, and in many other areas cannot be denied.

There is a great lesson to be learned from these facts, one that we must take hold of, use, and understand. This lesson is that the mind can be conditioned to extremes in the wrong way. This is a fact that we must understand and apply in our educational process. Anything that deals with altering mental attitudes is a concern of education.

The results achieved by the Germans, Russians, and Chinese in brainwashing coincide with the findings of our research to such an extent that we educators can no longer close our eyes to them; we must adopt and apply the good points of this technique.

Although brainwashing is practiced to some extent in the classroom, we do not control the mind enough, keep it sufficiently occupied, give it the proper motivation for our efforts to succeed. We are not exploiting the ego of our pupils, but we must learn to do so. We must learn to control the material that is being used to condition the mind and develop our techniques to the fullest extent.

Many of our mentally blocked and therefore slow students are being brainwashed daily at home, in school, and in the community in which they live with negative suggestions and actions. Many parents are so eager for their children to learn that they coerce, abuse, deny, and even defame them to the point of blocking their minds. It is sad that these same tactics are used in many schools and by many teachers; this is how they were conditioned to teach. They were never warned that they could damage the mind or block it by these methods.

If we could control the minds of our students to such extent that they had no experience of any other kind of treatment, we could use the brainwashing tactics of the Germans, Russians, and Chinese and we would not encounter mental blocks as such. However, this is not a wise or feasible policy in our society since such treatment would block the minds of our students because of the many factors that control their conditioning.

Punishment is a common method of mind conditioning that has been used by kings, dictators, governments, schools, and homes from the beginning of time. However, if the mind is to realize its full potential, it must be relaxed and receptive. We are no longer conditioning the mind to be a pawn for kings or dictators.

Some of the brainwashing that is going on today all over the world is the act of constantly defaming, never allowing anything to be settled, to keep fear in the minds of the world, to stir up or suggest trouble, to such an extent that the minds are kept occupied with this kind of thinking all of the time. This tends to program the minds so they will react or compute the way they want them to.

This art of brainwashing is being used among students, parents, teachers, administration, in all walks of life. The continued sniping at our schools, the unrestrained attacks on education and its academic philosophy, the educational theories in use by our schools are a form of brainwashing to the nth degree. The reason for this is that schools are important to all homes, to all parents, and to all politicians. Those who wish to cause trouble will strike at our schools first.

However, you must realize by now there is a reason. We must learn to understand these controversies and use them to our advantage. We must use the knowledge that we have about the mind and how it is conditioned in order to condition it to understand what is going on and why. This will take a lot of the sting out of much of the brainwashing that is going on today. One of the bad circumstances about brainwashing in our society today is that we have many very susceptible citizens screaming their heads off about conditions and they usually have little or no knowledge concerning them. They are easy to condition; they are being used without their knowing a thing about the facts.

10. SOCIOLOGY, OLD AND NEW CONCEPTS

The solicitousness of parents and teachers is the cause of many hours of anxiety. It has been the cause of many great social changes. However, for many generations it has been known that whom one sees, whom he associates with, the culture of his teachers, his friends, and his parents, what he reads and what he sees, become the end result. The mind that he develops always depends on how he cultivated it or how the cultivation of others took hold, and on the cultural background of every phase of his life.

For centuries students have been sent to the best schools, to noted teachers, to locations of culture, for their mind conditioning. Parents who could afford to send their children would do so; many who could not afford to send their children to places of culture would do so at great sacrifices. The formula for success was whom you knew, whom you played with, whom you studied with, what you saw and what you read and studied.

The formula for success of the past is still a good formula for the present; in fact, recent research has found it to be more important now than ever. Mind conditioning begins at birth. Some even go so far as to claim it begins before birth. However, from birth on, conditioning takes place.

Research carried out from 1958 to 1964 by the National Communication Laboratories explains the use of toys in mind conditioning. This research explains that "play-starved" children from the cradle on become slow learners. It is not the toy but the use of the toy that counts. The failure to provide many learning motivations and experiences and the development of poor play habits lead to inner anxiety when he enters school. This is caused when he finds his new inferior role, when he finds his self-image inadequate to cope with the problems of his class and his sense of security and belongingness dissipated. The constant sense of failure is the cause of failure and creates frustration.

The answer is not altogether in the kind of toys. It lies in the line of proper programming, training and sufficient challenge.

The programming of the mind is becoming a new concept, revolutionary in mass education outside of school, and is now finding its way into many schools across the nation. Education has a lot to learn about programming its subject matter; teachers must learn how to use positive conditioning. The mind (computer) must be programmed from birth. This brings to mind a quote by Francis Keppel, Commissioner of Education, "Education must make good on the concept that no child within our society is either unteachable or unreachable—that whenever a child appears at the doors of our schools he presents a direct challenge to us and to all our abilities. For education, the question is not the environment that children bring to the school from the outside, but the environment the school provides from the inside."

A knowledge of what will result from proper environment and association has been available for thousands of years. To prove this, all one needs to do is pick up one of the great books of the great philosophers, such as Socrates or Plato. The following are a few such examples.

In the *Memorabilia of Socrates,* Chapter 1, Paragraph 20, you will find "For which reason fathers keep their sons, though they be of a virtuous disposition, from the society of bad men, in the belief that association with the good is an exercise of virtue, that association with the bad is the destruction of it." One of the poets also bears testimony to this truth, who says, "From good men you will learn what is good, but if you associate with the bad, you will lose the understanding which is in you." (environment)

In the Republic of Plato, Book 10, you will find: "In all these, now, does the man agree with himself, or as he disagreed with reference to sight, and had contrary opinions in himself of the same things at one and the same time, does he in the same manner disagree likewise in his actions, and fight with himself?" (self image)

Psychology has treated our environment in many ways, and in many cases the works of Socrates and Plato. A good example of this is the book *Talks to Teachers on Psychology* by William James (1922, Henry Holt and Company, New York). The evolution of psychology, of education, and mind conditioning has taken many turns to the right and to the left. However, the research of the past few years explains how and why the mind is conditioned.

There are many sociological and psychological aspects that will have to be studied, concepts of mind conditioning as a computer, and the use of proper programming in the home, school, and community. Every teacher must keep in mind many goals, the factors of positive and negative conditioning, the students' environment, cultural background, and make plans to improve each and every step.

Schools of today are being called upon to care for the economic, political, and social changes of our nation. These changes have been caused by our educational desires and teaching. The desegregation of our schools, the changes in the class and culture of our schools, the economic backgrounds of our students and parents will call for a giant killer program if we are to be successful with the education of our children.

The schools of the United States must set up values to strive for; these values must consist of developing a higher culture, the bringing of lower class standards up to those of the middle class. Education must not be caught in a dilemma, to strive or not to strive, for the values it sets. The schools of the United States must reach and obtain full status in American society; we must develop that society if the social changes of our nation are to be successful.

Education must grab the opportunity that is at hand; it must be very aggressive with its plans and set up an educational program that will meet the needs of all citizens. We must work as if we have only one class. We must work as if there were but one social background and must program the education in our schools to bring all society to a higher level. Each and every society in our nation has a lot to offer. Education can control the society of our nation. Therefore, education must decide the road to take and program it into the schools of our nation.

The plight of the American Negro is more than housing, lack of training, slums, poverty, etc. It extends to the genetic theory, which is the history of what has happened to them over a period of time. The Negro of today who lives in the ghetto has had less direct personal contact with the white life than any other generation in the American Negro history. Genetic research many years ago brought out facts that hold true with the Negro today as it has with animals and plants.

The laws of heredity or genetics have gone through the greatest biological revolution since World War II. The importance of genetics is that it follows a conventional and chronological pattern. The concepts of DNA and RNA (or moleculor genetics) must be extensively considered.

Mutation is a heritable change in the genetic material; a mutant is the changed organism that results. The variations are called mutant. Mutated elements have been localized in regions of chromosomes and even within the DNA. Genetics is coming to grip with the analysis of heredity at the molecular level.

The outstanding research of genetics and its results are important for long range planning for the Negro. The expected results of each action taken by our nation, schools, etc., can be foretold. What Mendel did with the pea plant, and what is known today concerning transmission of hereditary factors, illustrate the basic principles that have caused the plight of the Negro today, in fact the plight of many whites.

The fact is, the Negro as a whole must be commended for not having a bigger breakdown than actually exists. However: science and education can help with the planning of future events.

Their problems are the results of defecting planning, of slavery, of freedom without plans to integrate, educate, etc., therefore their plight grew worse instead of better. Religion, morals, education, family relations, responsibilities, etc. were not a part of their newly found freedom. Existence was their prime factor then as it is today.

Genetic research has brought out many facts but one of its most important findings is the carryover from the parent. The size, height, color, build, sensitiveness and many other qualities are carried over from the genes of the parent. From this knowledge plants and animals have been improved with outstanding success. It is known that the genes carry a certain pattern and have a lot to do with the abilities and desires. Past generations have a great bearing on the future. More so with the Negro and poorer class of people than most scientists wish to admit.

Negroes have spent generations of time where they have been dominated, where the male was not responsible for a home; he was not taught to do more than a very few things. The responsibility of a home or family was not included.

The Negro woman, however, was taught to care for the home, trained to cook, sew, plan for childbirth, raise their children, and in many cases were educated so they could read and write and teach the children of her master. To a great degree, these same conditions continued to exist after they gained their so called freedom. The Negro women are the ones who have been most successful. They have been able to learn, hold jobs and care for their children. They have more desire to rise above their present status than the men, all due to their past training.

Most Negro women have no desire to be married to a Negro man whom they would have to support. Most Negro men would not know how to care for a middle class home, nor would he have the desire to keep it that way if it were given to him, with the finances to keep it as he received it.

These are facts that the nation must face when it makes its plans to help the Negro out of his plight. These ills will not be overcome quickly, it will take generations (and even then) we will have the weak. Evidence of this comes from what is called the throwback. With registered animals that have gone through generations and generations of breeding, throwbacks show up. The remedy is not what Hitler tried to do, weed out the weak, and develop the strong. The weak can be developed, the strong can be made stronger. Through proper mind conditioning, a successful change can be accomplished.

There is one factor in the favor of the Negro that has been overlooked by most. The Negro went through generations of breeding to obtain a better worker. Genetically this is in his favor. The Negro with push and drive, who escaped to the North, who found work and a good home, became great.

The movement of the Negro to the big cities after World War II was so great that housing could not be made available. They moved into the slum areas and formed the present day ghettos; they lived together, the more they could cram into a house the better off they were. Survival was their objective. The children had to absorb the brunt of harsh punishment, loss of parental control, were yelled at, slapped, starved, beaten, and the consistent abuse and violence was enough to deprive them of the prequisite to learning. The negative conditioning that most of the Negro children from the ghetto had to contend with would have destroyed the best of the white. The damaging effects of being deprived of the nourishment of love, shelter, morals, etc. creates a student who is interested only in self preservation for the moment, with no ideas of the future. He is convinced he has no future, so why try.

Education has the job of re-conditioning the minds of the Negro. A positive outlook and desire must first be developed. Some of the requirements to start with are food and shelter; schools; teachers who are interested and willing to work on a positive basis; jobs and training for the parents; guidance clinics; psychiatry for certain parents and children; health clinics and much more. However, education has the biggest job. A mind can be reconditioned, therefore the Negro can be helped. How much depends on how well it is planned and carried out.

11. SOME OF THE RESEARCH EXPLAINED

Most research is explained through case histories; however, some reports are more intelligible when they are literary in nature. A great amount of insight can be obtained from each method of reporting. Therefore, both arrangements are used.

I found through the use of hypnosis in programming the mind that if I programmed a statement on the mind that was not true, to overcome this impression or correct it, I had to repeat the correct statement more than once. The truth was also found that nothing is ever erased from the mind, no matter how often one is told that the statement is not true. All that one needs to do is ask the subject, "What was it I said that was not true?" and he will tell you. Therefore, an impression is not erased; it is overcome by other associated facts.

An impression made through deep concentration is much harder to overcome than one that is made lightly. The act of telling the subject that he will not remember this statement again will not clear it from his mind. It will, however, keep his mind from computing it for a time. The act of telling a subject that he will not remember is an act of blocking his mind. Blocks will at times let go, circuits will repair themselves, and the mind may in time respond to the impression that was thought to have been cleared.

The fact then remains that once an impression has been made, even though it has been overcome, it still remains in the mind. If the mind is not computing properly, there is nothing to keep it from computing the wrong answers. The deeper the concentration is, the more crossfiling takes place. When an impression is overcome, no one can be sure that it was overcome in all the areas in which it was originally crossfiled. If the mind is not computing properly, it may compute false impressions that were thought to be overcome, or it may compute from another area not conditioned by the original impression.

Another experiment used was to give a student a statement to write and read; then, after a day, he was asked to write the statement again. The results were, that 100% of the twelve-year-olds could rewrite it, about 80% of the ten-year-olds could also, but the percent grew smaller as the age decreased. However, 100% of all the students could do so if they were conditioned to the sentence in the trance state.

In these controlled experiments, many factors were present and had to be present, if the experiments were to be conducted. The student has to know that an experiment was being conducted; he had to be conditioned to hypnosis (which increased his ability to concentrate). They understood their mind and how it functioned better, they wanted to please, and they told us how the mind is conditioned to respond under normal conditions.

One's subconscious mind is very sensitive when one is in a deep trance, more so than normal. In fact some of the things that a conditioned person can do are almost beyond the imagination. One of these unbelievable acts which is very hard to understand is to have a very susceptible student listen to a tape played at 7.5 speed but recorded at 3.75 speed, while under deep hypnosis. The student will be able to tell you everything that is on the recording and at times will be able to do so when it was recorded at 1⅞ speed. I have never found one individual able to come even close to this feat without first having some mind conditioning with hypnosis.

Another test to show you how very sensitive the mind can be while it is under hypnosis, is to place the subject on the far side of a room and tell him that he will be able to hear you whisper to someone on the other side of the room. You then whisper so very softly that the person you are whispering it to cannot hear. Then ask the subject to repeat what you said; in most cases the subject can do so. The more he practices the faster he can respond.

There are many more such experiments and all have about the same results. What these experiments really show is that the mind and senses become very sensitive when under hypnosis, but what is important is that the mind can be conditioned to be almost as sensitive without the said trance state. However, to reach this state, a lot of conditioning must take place. One must be conditioned to believe in himself. He must then be conditioned to want to accomplish the act. He must be conditioned to concentrate. He must have a feeling of success. He must have the energy and drive, and work at the required assignment. He must be relaxed, with all pressures released, and learn to clear his mind of all interfering thoughts. These are the main points of conditioning the mind, but other elements of less importance will become very evident.

The power of perception, the practice or the art of disciplining the mind, the art of listening, of reading, of speech are all agents in learning. However, to gain a very sensitive mind so that all the processes of learning will take place, a student should concentrate on the following: I have a very powerful and sensitive mind. My mind is going to become more and more sensitive. I will remember everything that I hear. I will remember everything that I read. My memory is getting stronger and stronger. My mind will generate a tremendous amount of energy. All the mental blocks in my mind are draining out and letting go. All the nerve circuits in my mind and body will be active and sensitive. I am going to enjoy learning new things. I will like school. I will understand negative statements and they will not bother me or cause mental blocks. I am going to feel good. I am going to rest at night and be rested all day. My mind will be clear and it will be very sensitive. I am going to understand how my mind functions and I will use it properly. I will never think negatively. I will learn to concentrate and develop problems for my subconscious mind to compute for me. I will be expecting an answer and I will recognize the answer when it comes.

There is no doubt these methods can be improved upon in many ways. There are many other important elements to be considered, such as happiness, etc.

Students should be trained to understand their minds; there should be classes to train them how to use their minds, how to think to obtain the greatest results, to understand positive and negative conditioning, etc.

The attitude of the student concerning himself will change, his disposition toward teachers, parents, and friends will improve, for he now understands why certain reactions take place as they do.

We as teachers must remember that the attitudes of our nation, the emotions of groups of people and those of the churches stem from the mind conditioning of its citizens. Attitudes are conditioned the same as the students' thoughts are conditioned. The temperament of a child is easily swayed and conditioned; his mind can be conditioned in many, many ways. However, the most important factor in conditioning his mind is what he hears and sees.

The social aspects of mind conditioning reach into the far corners of the earth, from East to West, and from North to South. Our schools have the keys to open the doors to a great and wonderful society, our country has the chance to open the doors to the world, through proper mind conditioning. These doors must be opened on a positive conditioning. Negative conditioning through fear and hate will never help open the doors of the world to a good social change. The classroom teachers hold the future of the world in their hands, the kind of society we will have.

Teachers must remember they too have a very wonderful mind, with no limit to its accomplishments. The abilities of the teachers are great and varied and should be used to their utmost. The importance of your abilities as they relate to the future of education is beyond the imagination. However, the conclusions of this report reflect the reasons why there are so many unhappy teachers, why they have negative attitudes and poor image. Teachers have been conditioned through negative processes the same as others and many are very susceptible.

At times, success in teaching is hard to measure. Good teachers, however, know when their students are learning well, even the degree or rate of the learning which is taking place. (This is why I know you will recognize the success of positive mind conditioning.) The good teacher enjoys his students and is pleased when he sees his students mature; he is pleased when he has a part in the mind conditioning and has a great feeling inside of success as he observes the growth. The dedicated teacher is a successful teacher, happy, relaxed and full of energy and drive.

This report, I hope, will cause the individual teacher to do a lot of inductive thinking and reasoning. There is a need for a set of general principles to cover the process of positive mind conditioning. However, many conclusions in many particular situations will be found to be deductive reasoning, for you will accept the reasons and conclusions when you observe that the actions and results take place. The need for the great abilities and wisdom of the teachers to continue all types of reasoning with mind conditioning is a necessity for future gains in education. The implications of this report reach into many areas, for to start a research program in a small part of the process beyond this report would take a great force in every field of endeavor upon the globe. When you speculate on this subject, you will find your mind computing and reasoning for you and will call upon your intuition in many cases.

The fact that psychology or mind conditioning is not a true or real science is the reason why many hypotheses and conclusions become indirect, but as you observe proper mind conditioning, the formation of parallel postulates seems to fall in place.

Every teacher should have a part in extending the research, for by working with it you will become a part of it, you will find yourself so engrossed with hypotheses and conclusions, with excitement of success, that you will find yourself skipping over the high spots and not examining the others, you will find that there isn't time to waste on details.

The years prior to this research resulted in many turns to the right and to the left, it found me trying to tie the results to modern psychology, then an attempt was made to develop a psychology to fit the process with its own hypotheses and conclusions. However, to keep our research from growing stale, I decided to make a report to the public and to ask them to help with the never ending details, to let the teachers have this wonderful method to use now, for our classrooms are all laboratories and with so many great minds working in unison, more could and will be done. (Your conclusions will be interesting.) However, the real conclusions are that it works, there are reasons for its success, everyone can use it, it is easy to accomplish.

I am giving you a very wonderful and workable process or method (to use in your classroom); also, I have given you an understanding of your own mind and abilities and the "why" of many things. The full, positive mind conditioning will take years of research to accomplish and the help of you, the home, and the community is a must.

12. CASE HISTORIES

The process of checking my case histories and deciding which to report on becomes a dilemma, for I keep thinking back a few years to some of the subjects I had right after I realized what I was really doing. The reason why some of these remain in my mind so well is that the process of mind conditioning was new and the phenomenon of such success was overwhelming.

I was proud of my success, but even so the negative thought kept running through my mind, the next subject won't respond, he just can't. I was full of doubt, very negative with my thoughts about the possibilities of being successful; in fact, I was very negative with many of my thoughts.

I was willing to try with any kind of a case, which developed a varied folder of case histories. Success drove me to volunteer my services; I would ask and at times beg permission to work with the subject. Receiving pay for my services was the farthest from my mind. I am ashamed to admit the desire to help someone was not the driving force, the urge to experiment with another case drove me on.

Some of my early subjects did not impress me. They became outstanding students, but the change in their pattern of learning did not seem to really sink into my mind as being important. It was while I was in the armed services that the big impact came to me. It was then I had time to think back on or about the results. The desire came to me to learn more about mind conditioning, also about the process of hypnosis. From then on, the days were not long enough for I spent all of my extra time in work and study.

The results of the study became very important data that I wished to share with my friends. However, educators, psychologists, and friends in the field thought my ideas were far-fetched and impossible. Their advice to me was to quit and forget. I soon quit talking about what I was doing but I kept right on working. It was not until the time that I developed the process of self-hypnosis for the students that my friends began to realize that I was getting results. Their encouragement came when it was needed most.

Those early cases caused me to spend many a sleepless night thinking about what really was happening. I awoke many nights dreaming about the case and many times would go to my study and write about it. I now wish to share with you some of the information about a few of these early cases and you will see why I could not quit and forget.

One of the subjects was a 13-year-old boy who could not read or write his own name. He had spent all of his school days in a special class for the retarded. The boy was a very nice looking young man, he liked all kind of sports and could do quite well with them when he was given the chance. He liked to visit and talk about many things, but when school and studies were mentioned he would show fear and hate and would tell everyone at once he was too dumb to learn.

I will give this boy the name of Wilbur for the sake of writing about him. Wilbur had an older brother who had an I.Q. above 140; a younger brother with an I.Q above 140; his I.Q. was below 65. The father was a highly educated man with a Ph.D. degree, his mother had a B.A. degree.

When I met Wilbur's father to discuss his school work, his father explained that Wilbur was dumb, so dumb that he would never be able to read or write his name.

He explained to me that he had known for years how dumb his son was, also that there was no hope for him for they had done all they could for him. He asked us to do our best with him, that that was all he could ask. It was very easy to see that he was ashamed to even have to talk about him. Wilbur's father was very concerned as to what he would be able to do when he grew up to be a man, but he was very certain nothing could be done for him, thus he did not want to be bothered.

This is one of the cases where I asked to work with the subject, then begged to work with him, to the point that the father became angry with me and asked me not to return to their home.

I was so sure that Wilbur was blocked so he could not learn, for when I wrote his name on a piece of paper and asked him to copy it, his arm became rigid. When I would point to his name and ask him to read it, he would look and look at the word and then look up at me and ask, "What word?"

I attended a party a few days before Wilbur came to my school. This party was attended by a number of world-famous hypnotists. Each of them had brought one of his outstanding subjects along so that they could demonstrate some of their processes, also so that they could have a chance to work with each other's subjects. One of the things that was demonstrated that night by one of the hypnotists was to condition my subject so that he could not see me when he was brought out of the trance. It was fun to watch him look all over for me and he kept saying, "He went home without me" yet, I was standing right in front of him. He asked one of the men (who lived close to his home) to let him ride home with him.

This act was a mental block placed in his mind. He acted just like Wilbur when he would look at his name on a paper and then say: What word? Wilbur's father kept telling me, when I would discuss the possibilities of his being blocked: "He couldn't be blocked, for he has never been hypnotized." However, after so long a time and after much pestering, he gave in and told me to work with his son in any way I cared. When the chance came for me to work with Wilbur, I almost backed out, for I knew that a failure now would be a blow to my ego and to my theories on mind conditioning.

Success was almost beyond words to describe. Wilbur could see the words and his name, he could copy his name and he acted as if he were going to explode with joy. He seemed to know at once that he could now learn, whereas before he was convinced that he could not.

Within the one school year he caught up with his class. Of his own free will he would stay after school and study until the teacher went home. He would beg the teacher to stay longer and help him. His father, mother, and older brother helped him at home with his school work. The mother became perturbed because she had to turn the light out on him to get him to sleep. Wilbur became a very outstanding student and continued to be one.

Some of the history about Wilbur and why he became so blocked is very interesting. The cause of his block, I am sure, is the cause of many other students' becoming blocked with their school work. Wilbur did not walk until he was over two years old, he did not talk until later than that. The father and mother were convinced that he was dumb and that he had something wrong with him. The belief of the father was that he should know he was slow or dumb, therefore he told him over and over how dumb he was and after he started to school and could not learn his own name at once, his father told him; "Son don't worry, it's all right, you will never be able to read and write your name but we love you".

Need I say more about the case? Wilbur was blocked. His father came to me and cried like a baby and said "My God, my God, I almost ruined my own son". I wish to say that without special help he would have ruined his own son.

Remember now, Wilbur's father said that Wilbur had never been hynotized. Had he? I think he had.

13. NEGLECT

The problems of conditioning the mind depend on how the mind is used. The mind must be kept busy, thoughts must be controlled, the programming of the mind with ideas and facts must be carefully designed in order that interfering thoughts may not have time to creep in.

If a computer is neglected and facts are not programed upon its brain, nothing will be computed from it that is worthwhile. The mind is the same; through neglect it will deteriorate, it will become subliminal to past programming.

The next case history is about a boy whom I will call Steve. When Steve was twelve years of age his I.Q. was 60. He had been kept in a special class for the retarded most of his school years. He was almost a non-reader. His disposition was one of unhappiness, dejection, and somnolence. Steve's plans were to stay in school until he was sixteen, then join the Merchant Marine.

Steve was born in New York City. His mother died giving birth to a brother one year younger than he. There were two older children. The father was a college graduate and after the war obtained a very good position. The mother was a college graduate. Since the father had to be away from home most of the time to keep his job, he could not keep a home established after the death of his wife. He found a home for all of his children with relatives except for Steve. Steve was boarded out from place to place until he was five and started to school. At this time he was boarded out with a very old couple, the man was 75 and the lady was 72. Both of these folks worked part-time, but their working hours were so arranged that someone was home at all times. These folks were almost non-readers; the man dropped out of school when in the fourth grade and the lady quit school when she was in the eighth grade.

Records show that Steve was an average student when he was in kindergarten and the first grade but failed the second grade and was held back a year. When Steve was held back to repeat the second grade, he was put in the special class for the retarded. From this point on, Steve spent most of his time in special classes. When Steve was in the fourth grade, he was boarded out with another old couple since sickness demanded a change. Steve not only changed homes but changed schools. The new environment was worse on Steve than the old, for the school he attended did not have special classes for the retarded. He was placed in an average fourth grade with a teacher who believed she could pound knowledge into the heads of her students.

Steve was denied use of the playground for he had to report to the classroom and study when he arrived at school. He ate his lunch in the classroom and was kept after school each night to study. His foster parents belief was the same as that of the teacher. Therefore, he was denied the right to play at home and spent most of his time in his room. He was kept in his room to study, but no one would help him.

Steve's father came to visit him at Christmas time and saw what was happening and took him to a boarding school for boys. Steve spent the next few years in this boarding school. He was rejected by both students and teachers and soon had the nickname of dunce. Dunce was being used freely by the students and teachers when an aunt stopped in to visit him. Steve was twelve years of age and about the size of one of her sons. She became so furious with what she saw and heard that Steve was taken out of this school and brought to her home in California.

This took him away from the school and placed him in a very wonderful environment. There were two boys in the home close to his age, one a bit younger and one a little older. There was a heated swimming pool, a large yard, lots of books and playthings.

Steve learned to swim, learned to play with his new friends, and became one of the family. He learned to like his new home, respected everyone there, and wanted to please them. However, when school started the next fall he was in trouble, bad trouble. Exams showed that he could not fit into their program, for he could not read. He was again placed into a special class for all subjects. However, this time conditions were different. He had a very understanding aunt and a school that was willing to do anything to help him. After a couple of months of school and no real progress, his aunt called me in to work with Steve. (His aunt's family understood positive conditioning for I had worked with members of this family in the past). With their cooperation and my work with Steve a great change took place. He learned to read. Within six months Steve had almost caught up with his class. Steve knew that he was learning at a very rapid pace. Success and desire drove him on and it became unquenchable.

I will never forget the night when I invited a very good friend to my home to observe my work with Steve. This friend was chairman of the education department of a state college. I often asked for help, advice, and constructive criticism. We often exchanged ideas and views about mind conditioning.

This meeting took place after I had worked with Steve for quite some time. He was no longer somnolent but a very wide awake young man. After I had worked with Steve and he became awake, my friend asked him some questions. One of these questions had to do with what Steve now thought about his ability to learn. Steve's answer took my friend aghast, for he stood up and said, "I am now a brain, I can learn anything. School is easy and I enjoy it now." He said, "Physically and mentally I was numb but now I feel alive all over, it's just like walking out of a dark room into daylight." (I have had other students make this same statement.)

The consciousness of Steve and of many other subjects like him substantiates neglect as an agent of destruction to learning. The cause of apathy setting in with Steve was the lack of toys, playmates, help, and advice, and his being made to mope.

This case is no exception, for after I started working with deep mind conditioning, I have found like cases everywhere.

14. READING

When I think about reading and the art of teaching reading, a very special case comes to my mind. Learning to read is, at times, a very complicated process. The destructive power of a student's emotions all too often will block them. Learning to read becomes a tremendous force of evil if the student is not conditioned and prepared before the teaching takes place. The preparation must continue, conditioning must be a part of each day's lesson if the student is to learn well. Negative emotions, such as bitterness, envy, and hatred, creep into the process both at home and in school.

Parents' desires, envy, and ego at times become a force of destruction. Parents' efforts to teach their children the reading skills before the student has been conditioned to read often stimulate negative conditioning.

The old belief or assumption that a child must be ready to read before he can be taught to read is true; however, he may be conditioned and made ready. The other old assumption that parents should not do the actual teaching of reading skills is not true, for a very high percentage of reading skills are taught by the parents. Parents have a very important part in the reading skills, that is the part of preparation, the part of encouragement, to stimulate, and then keep proper materials for the children to browse through. It is important to read stories to a child. While reading, pictures should be shown that fit the story; field trips or shopping trips may become wonderful learning experiences. Then when they begin to ask about words and their meanings, help them, but do not push.

The case that fits this picture is one of a young girl

15 years of age, in high school and a non-reader. There was no doubt about her ability; she was very receptive, she could remember what anyone would read to her but just could not read.

I had this student in a 9th-grade arithmetic class. She could not do the multiplication tables above the fives without making marks and then adding them up. However, when she was given a copy of them written out to the twelves and then made to copy over the set and say them as she copied them, she soon learned them. From then on, if someone would read the problem to her, she could work the problem. Her teachers would give her an oral exam and she would end up with good grades.

When this girl was in the 10th grade I started working with her with deep hypnosis. She was taught self-hypnosis but was not practicing it at home. For six weeks very little progress was evident. She felt better but said she just didn't have time to practice. However, when her mother found out that she should be working on self-hypnosis, she saw to it that time was made available. Within the next six weeks she advanced so that she could read most all of her school work. Of course, she was very slow at first but her speed became better as she practiced. Within another six weeks she could read all of her school work and understand it. Her understanding of words was normal before she learned to read.

When I checked into some facts about her early training in reading skills, I discovered a very common negative condition which is found in many homes. Her father was a literati, an editor, and an outstanding writer. His ego and his desire caused him to believe that his daughter was a genius and that he would prove it by teaching her how to read and write at two and a half years of age.

The drama that took place in this home (as in many others) became one of sarcasm, hate, and rebellion. The scolding, spanking, and rebuttal led to divorce. A mental block had been induced and interfered with the learning of a very intelligent child. This girl might well enough have been a genius. Had this father spent his time conditioning his daughter to want to read and making it a wonderful desired experience, he would have been successful.

Before I end this case I wish to explain one thing. When I had this girl under hypnosis, I did not teach her one word or try to do so. I kept telling her that she would want to read, that she could read, and that the next time she picked up her book she would recognize the words and be able to read them. She knew the words and their meanings.

15. STORED-UP EMOTIONS

Another very interesting case history, and one of my very first cases where hypnosis was used for the good of education, is about a boy in high school who had been a very outstanding student but began failing all of his subjects. The reasons for my explaining this case to you are (1) to show that emotions will change the pattern of thinking and abilities to learn, (2) stored-up emotions, at times, will jump out at us to such an extent that they will cause mental disorders that cannot be controlled by the subject.

This boy was in one of my high school classes and was failing. He was also or had been one of the best basketball players on my basketball team. Since all of his teachers had reported him failing their classes, he was ineligible for sports until he brought his grades up to an average.

For eleven years, this student had maintained above-average grades. He had won his letters in high school basketball and track. His older brother and sister were college graduates. He was a member of the Boy Scouts and had worked his way up to where he had more honors than any other Scout in his troop. He had been a very happy-go-lucky type of an individual, well liked by all of the students and teachers.

I will give him the name of Bill in order that I may write about him with a name.

When he was in the twelfth grade Bill came to school a very changed boy. He kept to himself, seldom smiled, and never entered into school activities. He would sit in class with his head down, seldom opened a book, never handed in a paper or took part in class activities. He had lost weight and looked very unhealthy.

I had noted that while he was in my class, he seemed to have lost his hearing, for when I called upon him to answer a very easy question, he would not hear his name called or know that I called upon him to recite. Other teachers reported encountering this same situation in their classes.

Bill and I had a number of meetings after school during which we talked about his actions and what was happening to him. He would cry and say, "Please don't bother me, I am doing as well as I can." However, Bill would never talk about the reasons, no matter how hard I pressed him.

I knew Bill's older brother and sister but did not know anything about the family history. When I checked to find out more about him, I found that he was living with his sister and her husband on a farm.

I made a visit to his sister's home one day to talk to her and her husband about Bill, when I knew Bill would be gone. His sister reported that Bill was a wonderful boy but had changed so much. Neither of them knew what could be wrong. They had him checked by a number of doctors and he seemed to be physically well, they had tried to talk to him and said he would clam up and would not respond. This change had taken place over the summer vacation months when Bill was helping them on the farm. At that time he liked farming and wanted to be a farmer. They asked him if he wanted to quit school, but he said "no."

Then is when I asked about his father and mother. I was told a very great tragedy had taken place when Bill was 4 years old. They said that Bill had been a witness to this tragedy but that this surely could not have a bearing on him now, for he was the first one of the family to forget it.

When I had a chance to see Bill alone, I called him

into my classroom and asked him point blank if this could have a bearing on his condition. I thought by being blunt, by doing it quickly before he had a chance to set up a defense, he might let me know; he did. He broke down and sobbed for one entire period and told me through his tears, "Yes, I dream about it every night, my mind is tied to it all day long, I am so dazed with it I do not know what I am doing."

This is when I thought of hypnosis. Would I dare use it on him? Then I remembered his Scout Master was a young minister, who knew about hypnosis, for he and I had used it at a Sunday School party. I talked to him about Bill and explained to him what I had found out about his troubles. He also thought about hypnosis and asked me, "Why don't we work with him."

After the second exposure to hypnosis, Bill underwent a wonderful change. He looked rested, he began to work in school, he took up with his old friends, and was on his way to being his old self. We worked with him over a period of four weeks, seeing him once a week after three meetings in the first week.

Bill continued to improve, graduated from high school, spent a stretch in Military Service, and returned. He is now a very successful married business man with his own business, and a very wonderful family.

This is one of the cases that caused me to concentrate about the use of hypnosis and education when I was in the Armed Services.

School records show there are many students who maintained good school standards for a long period of time and then became hopeless as students and citizens. I have found over a period of time that many citizens, both young and old, become entangled with emotions that existed when they were quite young, emotions that seemed to have cleared with no ill effects but jumped out of their past to change them. Why their mind (computer) plays back to them these great emotions is unknown, but it is known that this changes their pattern of computing or thinking.

I find many factors that cause negative mind conditioning; just a few of these are neglect, scorn, emotional dramas from pressure, the continued telling a student that he is dumb, the student's belief and his continued thinking that he is inferior, and many more which I have listed in my book.

To have you believe that all the students that I worked with become good and wonderful would be a great injustice. There are a few that I could not reach for they refused even to see me. They refused to try to help themselves. Maybe I should cite a case or so to show you what I am talking about.

A boy aged 16 who came to my home with his father to see me is one. This boy had been an average student. He was in the 11th grade in school and was failing all his subjects. He wanted to quit school and go to work. He did not want to see me or talk about his school work.

He called his father many names and interrupted him continually throughout the interview. He agreed to come to me for help if he could have the car to drive one night a week. The father told me that the boy was out until after midnight every night, that at times he would not return home after school but stayed out until he got ready to come home. (There is much more to this case than what I am listing.) The student came six or seven times and would only talk. He would take no part in hypnosis or self-hypnosis.

Another case is about a boy who had been in a number of schools. He had an older brother and a younger sister who were outstanding in school. His father and mother were well educated and desired to help their son. Continued pressures at home kept the boy upset to the point of not wanting to even try to please. However, he started out very well, his grades came up to average, his attitude was good, and he was working with himself through self-hypnosis. Then a teacher at his school scorned him over and over in front of the class. His parents took up the chant at home, "You have proven to us you can do the work," they would say, "so now—you're going to do so." Thus a good start was lost.

I have a list of five students who received very little help. The five represent about 1% of the total.

16. HOMEROOM STAR

You will notice that homeroom has been given a star; it should have a group of stars since it is so important to the school, the student, and the home. It is important to other classroom teachers if it is used as it should be.

The homeroom was organized to take the place of the large study halls, to give a hand with guidance, to help the student with his problems, and to have a means of home contact. A homeroom must fit the local needs, local ideas and traditions, age, grade, maturity, and judgment and still allow leeway and freedom for individual changes. Their activities should start small and then expand. Too many committees and activities all at once will complicate the program.

For the high school (both junior and senior), students should stay with the same teacher while they are going to this school. The teacher should organize the room in various ways with its officers and committees.

Each homeroom teacher should make out and keep a set of records on each student; these records should be kept current at all times. Some of them will be records that will not be found in the school accumulative file, along with information from the guidance accumulative file of the school. These records will be used to help the student and provide information for other teachers who will need it. You will be able to know the student better since this information will help you counsel the student as he needs it.

The information will help when you and the parent work together on a problem. Most of all, it will help you understand the student's problems well enough so that you both can work together on them. This will give you and the school some holding power of the student and will help to keep him from becoming a push-out, or drop-out, or whatever may be the name for it.

More can be accomplished through a good homeroom, when the homeroom teacher is actively doing a good job of helping and protecting his students than anywhere else in the entire school system. A homeroom is a place to study, a place to obtain help with school work, to meet fellow classmates, pursue activities, and most of all a place where a student can *go for help* on any problem and *get help*.

The records on file in the homeroom should contain a copy of his program, his report cards, unsatisfactory slips, records of any serious physical handicaps, interests, information about his home, his parents and where they work, the name of the family doctor, activities of the home, activities he is in at school, and many facts. *You should know the student.* Be sure that the student knows that you are willing to help him with any problem.

Guidance Aspects

A. The purpose of the homeroom is primarily guidance for the student. The homeroom teacher may best know his pupils through the use of:

1. Elementary cumulative records (known as *cums).*
2. Test data.
3. Anecdotal records (check-up sheets, conferences, unsatisfactory slips, and vice-principal's notes).
4. School grapevine (know something about the pupils' own world and languages).
5. Home calls.

a. Prepare pupils and parents.
b. Don't patronize

c. Look and listen.

d. Offer constructive sympathy, not pity.

e. Strive for a specific result.

f. Be friends; listen to confidential statements, without criticizing or laughing.

6. Actual counseling

a. Be sure pupil knows what you are counseling him for and why.

b. End conference with at least one specific plan for improvement.

c. Keep your word; insist that the pupil keep his.

d. Use your data.

e. Praise all accomplishments.

f. Give privacy; protect pride.

g. Help the pupil to understand the role of the classroom teachers.

7. A pupil must feel that you are on his side (and you must be). Cums follow pupils for years; use extreme discretion in writing damaging reports. Write significant summaries that will help future teachers.

B. *Discipline and the Homeroom*

1. Place responsibility on the class officers as soon as you can. Hold them accountable.

2. Insist that the class be quiet during the flag ceremony and bulletin announcements.

3. In talking to individuals, appeal to their better nature.

4. Discuss problems with physical education teacher.

5. Interview parents.

6. Call the attention of the vice-principal to the problem.

7. Use group pressure of peers.

8. Support the work of other teachers. Ask them to notify you if they are having trouble with a pupil in your homeroom.

9. Conduct a simple conference with other teachers of the pupil.

10. Discuss problems with a grade advisor. Check cumulative records.

11. Support your homeroom teams by enthusiastic attendance at their games.

12. Plan group social activities.

13. Talk to your homeroom group about its abilities.

14. Keep telling them how wonderful they are.

15. Be sure each homeroom period is planned.

Homeroom Procedures Recommended by Teachers

1. Project to help others—boxes of clothes to "displaced persons" and the needy.

2. Socioigrams—designed to place social misfits in a social atmosphere (where more positive conditioning can take place).

3. Guidance by the use of "National Forum Guidance Series."

4. Unsigned questions are submitted by the students. Discussion of these questions after you have checked them.

5. Homeroom bulletin board maintained by students' committee.

6. Know birthdays of each member of the room. Celebrate each month. Comment on great people born in same month.

7. Try to be in your room at least twenty minutes before the bell; admit your homeroom students and their friends.

8. Award something for prompt return of report cards, papers, etc. Award stars for participation in drives. The aim is 100% participation.

9. Visitation by students to other homerooms.

10. Class officers take roll. This builds responsibility.

11. History book—pictures of officers at each grade level, and of events.

12. Push school activities.

13. Our correspondence secretary sends get-well-quick cards to teachers and students who have been ill for several days.

14. Interview each student and the teacher who gave him a "U" to try to help solve problems. Pupils report on their progress.

15. Use of self-evaluation blanks.

16. Change their seats often in order that they may make friends easily.

17. Topic: "How I got my part-time job." Talks by students on vocational interests.

18. Have each pupil state at least one problem. These problems can be classified as personal, social, domestic, or scholastic.

19. Have a tutoring section for low grades or subject difficulty.

20. Junior and senior high school orientation for A.6's and A.9's.

21. Have the main topics for the day on the board before the homeroom session begins. This starts the pupils thinking and talking about the idea.

22. The number system for roll call saves valuable time for extra projects.

23. Have community singing on occasions.

24. Pupils bring reading and study materials to use during roll and while special committees are meeting.

25. Questionnaire: "Let's get acquainted."

26. Talent show and skits for homeroom drives.

27. Have many class officers.

28. Read articles on good grooming and dress.

29. Nail-biters come in early to work on nails. Nail box consists of cuticle sticks, emery board, cotton, etc.

30. Use "Tips to Teens" from the Sunday newspaper and "Sub Debs" articles for the girls homeroom.

You can add to this list; there are many, many things to do, but keep in mind that the homeroom has a reason and purpose. Remember that a successful teacher needs the education of a college president, the executive ability of a financier, the humility of a deacon, the adaptability of a chameleon, the hope of an optimist, the courage of a hero, the guile of a serpent, the gentleness of a dove, the patience of Job, the grace of God, and the persistence of the devil.

Drop-outs

The first indication of drop-out should appear to the homeroom teacher, and action to prevent it should be started at once. It is his duty to see that it never starts.

Drop-outs from school are due to a multitude of reasons, however, a high percent of drop-outs come from blighted neighborhoods where home and neighborhood conditions are disheartening. The root of most drop-outs stems from negative conditioning, for it is from these areas, where you will find the products of the past generation's negatively conditioned students, their parents.

Most of these drop-outs can be stemmed by the process of positive conditioning. The student can be conditioned to want to stay in school, to think something of himself, to believe in himself and then with a helping hand be given a chance to stay in school and make good. Keep him from being a "push-out."

Schools will need the help of all agencies; they must make contact and call upon all organizations to work with them.

A visit to some of these homes and neighborhoods tells a story so impressive that one wonders how the student has stayed in school and in the home as long as he has. This student needs help, advice, and someone to fall back on.

Drop-outs should cease if and when positive mind conditioning becomes a fact in schools and with the teachers.

HOMEROOM UNITS

UNIT I - GETTING ACQUAINTED

Autobiography Form

________________ (date).

A. Autobiography to be filled out by each student. (Required)

1. My name is ______________________________.

2. I was born on ______________ (month day year) in __________ (city), ________ (state).

3. My father's name is ______________________.

4. My mother's name is ______________________.

5. My brothers and sisters are:

(name)	(age)	(grade in school)
__________	______	__________
__________	______	__________
__________	______	__________

6. My father's work is ______________________.

7. My mother's work is ______________________.

8. The duties I have at home are ______________________

______________________________________.

9. On school days, I usually go to bed at __________ o'clock.

10. The subjects I liked best in elementary school were ____ ____

11. The subjects I like best in Junior High School are __________.

12. My best friends in school are ______________________.

13. I play the following musical instrument (s) ______________.

14. My favorite radio programs are ______________________.

15. My favorite television programs are ______________________

______________________________________.

16. My hobbies are ______________________________

______________________________.

17. I have an allowance. Yes ________ No ________

18. I earn my money by having a job ______________________.

19. I plan to go to college ______________________________.

20. I plan to work after I graduate from High School ______________.

21. I would like to be a member of Student Council ______________.

22. I would like to hold a homeroom office ________________.

23. I belong to the following clubs ____________________.

24. I am interested in belonging to these clubs ______________

______________________________.

25. I want to be a ________________________ when I grow up.

B. Getting acquainted with other members of the homeroom.
   1. Place the students in pairs or groups of not more than four. Try to put those from different elementary schools together. Each student of a group should learn as much as possible about the others. If desirabe, each group could, within a few days, give the rest of the class a "thumbnail sketch" of the students in that group. The groups could be rotated so that pupils could get to know a maximum number of others in the homeroom group.

C. Getting acquainted with other homerooms.
   1. Throughout the semester, try to combine forces with other homerooms for drives, games, and other activities.
   2. Have contest, such as "Personality of the week".

D. Getting acquainted with the school and teachers.

1. Each student should have a list of classes he is taking and be familiar with his teachers' names.

2. Each teacher with a new homeroom (new to the school) should take his homeroom students on a tour of the campus.

3. Have a chart in your homeroom, with the names of the administrators and coordinators listed, which indicates their positions and the locations of their offices. Have a map of the campus available which will show all the buildings and the location of the various offices (health,

You as a teacher can help yourself overcome habits by using a check list.

	Usually	Sometimes	Seldom
1. Am I honest with myself and others?			
2. Am I careful and accurate about details?			
3. Do I follow directions?			
4. Do I cooperate at play?			
5. Do I cooperate in the classroom?			
6. Do I cooperate at home with parents and students when I can?			
7. Am I kind and understanding?			
8. Am I dependable?			
9. Am I on time?			
10. Am I neat and clean?			
11. Am I thoughtful of others?			
12. Am I well mannered?			
13. Am I cheerful?			
14. Is my work completed?			
15. Have I been fair with my grading?			
16. Have I kept enough grades?			
17. Do I know each student well enough to grade him?			
18. Do I have a list of students whom I need to know better?			
19. Have I used my initiative and ambition properly?			
20. Am I thinking positive about myself?			

This is only a sample of a very few questions that should be asked and answered each day or as often as you can, until you are sure that you are being positive at all times.

attendance, counselor, business, bookroom, administration, etc.).

The use of the autobiography of the student as a school guidance technique has been a useful tool in many schools. The autobiography should be a "must" for each year. It should be systematically analyzed each year. The homeroom teacher will note the changes that take place in the student's preferences, his home, his abilities, his duties, etc.

The autobiographies will show the greatest attention to the family background; therefore, they must be used with professional care. Homeroom teachers will find the students making them longer each year, and by the time they are in high school, they become a personality inventory.

Unit II—Homeroom Organization

A. Suggested officers:

1. President
2. Vice-president
3. Secretary
4. Student Council representative.
5. Other officers may be important, such as sergeant-at-arms, welfare, etc.

Homerooms should require that all students who hold office maintain an average of "C" or an average grade.

B. Suggested committees.

1. Room beautification and cleanliness.
2. Ventilation.
3. Citizenship.
4. Fire drill captains.

5. Drives.

a. P.T.A. membership
b. Rag drive
c. Paper drive
d. Clean campus
e. Community Chest, polio, Red Cross, etc.

6. Health and welfare (sending cards to sick)
7. Committees for discussion units.
8. Safety committee.

9. In order that the students may learn correct parliamentary procedure, it is suggested that the homeroom be conducted under this procedure. Conduct all business at the beginning of the homeroom period.

Unit III—Orientation

A. Objectives for the homeroom

Every school system, and even schools within a system will differ. Therefore, any or all of the homeroom outlining in this book is only suggested; many schools will have a plan of their own. *Good homeroom organization is so important for positive mind conditioning* that we feel it very necessary to set up a skeleton homeroom program.

1. Feeling of belonging.
2. Leadership, initiative, and originality.
3. Good habits of citizenship.
4. Characteristics of courtesy, politeness and good manners.
5. School spirit and sportsmanship.
6. The feeling of working together as a team toward a common goal.
7. Good pupil-teacher relationship.
8. Good grooming.

9. One hundred percent participation.

B. Activities of the homeroom.

1. Official roll call.
2. Counseling.
3. School business.
4. Drives.

C. Units of discussion.

1. Orientation

a. Explanation of bell schedule.
b. Discussion of rules of the school.
c. Cafeteria procedures.

(1) Walk, do not run.
(2) Comb hair elsewhere
(3) Refrain from loud talking.
(4) Return trays.
(5) Choose food wisely.
(6) Conduct yourself courteously in lines.

d. Student store.

(1) Where located.
(2) When open.
(3) What is available.

2. Marks.

a. Subjects and their marks.

(1) How to get good marks.
(2) How to get an average mark.
(3) How to get poor marks.

(4) Explain that marks are recorded and kept on file and the purpose of such records.
(5) Employers' interest in good marks.
(6) How the grades are averaged by the teacher.

b. Citizenship Marks.

(1) Cooperation

(a) What it means.
(b) Importance on card.

(2) Work habits

(a) What it means.
(b) Importance of this mark.

c. Honor and scholarship.

(1) Explain to the students what it means, how to get on the list, how to qualify, and how important it is.

d. School clubs.

(1) Special interest clubs.
(2) After-school clubs.

Keep information on the bulletin board and often review requirements, meeting times, and events of the clubs.

4. Health office:

a. Where is health office?
b. When is doctor available?
c. When is nurse available?
d. What is to be done when someone is ill or injured?
e. Purpose of health office.

5. Counselor's office.

a. Where is counselor's office?
b. Duties of grade counselor.
c. Testing.
d. Programming.
e. Helping students with their problems.

6. Library procedures.

a. Where is the library?
b. Hours of the library?
c. How and when books may be checked out.
d. Have librarian talk to homeroom.
e. Library conduct.
f. Prompt return of books.
g. Fines.

7. Student council (if you have one)

a. How it operates
b. How it is formed.
c. Details of duties for council.
d. How to qualify.

8. Personal grooming.

a. Cleanliness.
b. Neatness of dress.
c. Brush teeth for health's sake.
d. Clean fingernails and hands.
e. Contest for best groomed boy and girl.

9. Courtesy.

a. Doing things the "nice" way.
b. "Courtesy is contagious"—slogan.

c. "It's so nice to be nice"—Sears' Slogan.

d. Take time to say "please" and "thank you."

e. Say "hello" and "good-bye" to your parents, fellow students, and teachers when you greet or leave them.

f. Call your teachers by name when you meet them. If you can say something pleasant to them, do so.

g. Review the importance of a pleasing personality and the qualities of a person.

10. Attendance.

a. Importance of good attendance.

b. Learning is improved as attendance is improved.

c. What to do when one is absent.

17. DO YOU KNOW HOW TO STUDY EFFECTIVELY?

Most students do not know how to study effectively; bad habits of study are responsible for many of their poor grades. The homeroom is the best place to teach the student how to study, and the best place to check with the student and parent on his homework. A study plan should be sent home to the parents, but they should be told that it is often a mistake to force their child to study when the rest of the family does. Let them know he may do better at another time. Have them try a number of plans before a set one is adopted. Remember to tell the parents to have a very relaxed study period. Tell them to remember that a study period should never become an emotional concern. Tell them it is better to drop the study period than to take the chance of negative mind conditioning. Explain to the parents what is meant by positive and negative conditioning and ask them for their help.

A study plan to present to the students and parents.

1. Do you plan your study?

a. Do you always plan to study at a certain time each day or evening?

b. Is this planned study period at a time when your mind works at its best?

c. Do you always use the *full* time? If your homework is completed, do you work on extra projects, reading, or review work?

d. Do you break long study periods with short periods of relaxing activities?

(1) Ten minutes is long enough for breaks. A long time makes it hard to settle down again. Breaks should take some form of physical exercise, such as stretching, walking around, having a snack, etc.

(2) Study periods of 15 minutes or less are not profitable for it takes that long to "warm up."

(3) Difficult material should be studied for periods of about 30 minutes. Plan to take breaks at good stopping places, such as the end of a chapter.

e. Do you plan the order in which you will spend your time studying, and how much time for each subject?

(1) Do you tackle your most difficult subject first?

(2) Do you set a time limit when you plan to be through with this subject?

f. Do you use a calendar to mark when notebooks and projects are due?

2. Is your study area right for effective study?

a. Is the area quiet without radio, television, or people to distract you?

b. Is there good lighting, ventilation, and proper room temperature in this area? (Example: a good light should be over the left shoulder, the temperature should be 70° F, and air circulation should be good. Do not face the light or work in a shadow or in sunlight.)

c. Is there a wide table or desk where there is room to spread out books and materials?

d. Is there a clock in view to help you follow your time budget?

e. Is your chair comfortable but not too soft?

f. Are all necessary study materials (pencils, paper, ruler, dictionary, etc.) always at hand?

g. At the close of your study period, do you straighten

up the study area so that everything is ready for the next day?

3. Do you make good use of your study time?

a. Do you thoroughly understand your assignments?

(1) Do you listen carefully to directions and write down all necessary information on the assignment page?
(2) Do you check on pages, numbers, titles, and problems required to see if you have copied them correctly on the assignment page?
(3) Do you ask questions about anything you don't understand?
(4) Do you start homework in class when given the opportunity?

b. Do you have all equipment on hand before you begin?
c. Do you begin studying immediately and keep your mind vigorous and active during the entire study period?
d. Do you try to do your work by yourself before you ask for help from your parents or other pupils?
e. Do you avoid all telephone calls or interruptions during the study periods? Have you told your friends (school friends) not to call at certain times?
f. Do you do only the required amount of work or do you tackle the additional assignments or look up new facts on your own?
g. When you complete an assignment, are you proud of it? Is it your best work? Is it neat, orderly, and thorough?
h. Do you know when to stop studying, especially if it is your bedtime? Try the work that has puzzled you first thing in the morning. Many great men have said: "I concentrate on the problem before going to bed and let my subconscious mind work out the problem for me while I

sleep." Try it; what someone else can do, you can do too.

i. Do you begin gathering materials immediately for your projects—then do something on them every week?

j. Do you use the library and reference books in a definite way to increase your knowledge of the subject?

k. Do you place finished homework and books in a definite place each night so that they are ready to take with you in the morning?

l. Do you know the power of suggestion will help you? Say to yourself: "I am going to get my homework, it is going to be easy, and I will understand it."

4. Do you keep a well organized notebook?

a. Do labeled dividers separate the work for each subject?

b. Do you keep an assignment sheet for each subject?

c. Do you write carefully so that you do not need to recopy your notes when you turn in your notebook?

d. Do you have extra notebook paper always on hand?

e. Do you reorganize your notebook periodically?

5. Do you know how to concentrate? Concentration is a habit which has to be developed by you in several ways. Concentration will be easier if you show interest and effort.

a. Do you *force* yourself to keep your mind on what you are doing? If your mind wanders, do you jerk it back immediately? (Useful device: Place a check mark on a piece of paper every time your mind wanders. Trying to keep down the number of marks helps to keep your mind on the work at hand.)

b. Do you ask yourself questions on the subject to bring your mind back to the lesson?

c. Do you sometimes read aloud to keep your mind from wandering?

d. Do you keep your mind active by retelling what you have read section by section?

e. Do you eliminate all distractions, or else force yourself to ignore noises on the radio and television and conversations in other parts of the house?

f. Do you prevent breaks in your train of thought by refusing to be interrupted by the telephone or by nibbling on snacks? Does the family respect your privacy? Do you keep thinking "I CAN"?

g. When writing a composition, do you start at once by making notes on ideas as they come to you? Then do you organize these ideas and write the material in its final form? (Don't wait for inspirations or writing moods. They may never come.)

h. Do you have a definite goal or purpose in mind so concentration will be more worthwhile?

i. Do you reward yourself for concentration during a work period? (A snack from the kitchen or a good television program *after study* may help as a reward.)

6. Do you need to improve your ability to remember what you read?

a. Do you have something definite in mind to look for as you read, such as (1) certain general information, (2) answers to specific questions, (3) solutions to the problems.

b. Do you glance rapidly at paragraph headings in the assigned material to get a general idea of the content?

c. To master the reading material, do you use the self-recitation method? (Retell in your own words what you have read.)

(1) After reading a paragraph or page carefully, close your eyes or the book and state in your own words the main points that you have read.

(2) If you can't do this, reread the page, looking for

definite points you wish to summarize, or makes notes of key words to remind you of what you wish to include. Another plan is to think of questions that you would like to have answered in each section; then read carefully, looking for answers to the questions.

d. Do you try to understand new important words in the reading assignment? Use the dictionary if you still do not understand the meanings of words after you have finished reading.

e. Do you read and study the charts, maps, tables, graphs, and illustrations in the textbook? These help you to summarize or visualize the material being read.

7. Do you read or need to read more rapidly and more accurately?

a. Ways to increase speed:

(1) Be determined to read faster.

(2) Have a definite purpose in mind for reading.

(3) Read more than one word at a glance. Force yourself to see phrases.

(4) Try to get the main thought in the paragraph, for two-thirds of the paragraph is usually devoted to an explanation of the main idea.

(5) Try not to move your lips or say a word to yourself. This slows your reading.

(6) Time yourself. See how much you can read in five minutes. See if the amount increases after a few days of concentrated work.

(7) Start practicing on easy, interesting fiction or magazine material to get the eye muscles trained to work more rapidly. Later, go on to more difficult material and continue reading it for six to eight weeks.

(8) Remember that reading rate varies according to whether the book is fiction or a textbook.

b. Do you read for enjoyment for a few minutes each day?

8. Are you accurate?

a. Do you always reread your compositions and written work, and check for capitalization, punctuation, correct spelling, and complete sentences?

b. Are your Latin, French, or Spanish words correct in form and spelling?

c. Are you accurate in your mathematics work?

(1) Do you read the problem carefully so that you understand exactly what you are to do?

(2) Do you think of the best and shortest way to solve the problem and work it carefully?

(3) Do you check each step of the completed problem for errors?

(4) Do you write all the numbers, letters, and signs distinctly?

(5) Are you careful to place decimal points correctly and to label answers?

(6) Do you have a special section in your notebook to record rules and formulas?

d. Do you study spelling carefully? Do you ever use the following method to study a word?

(1) Look at the word and pronounce it.

(2) Look at the word and use it in a sentence.

(3) Look at the word and say the letters.

(4) Close your eyes, picture the word, and say the letters.

(5) Cover the word and write it. Write it several times if it is not correct. Study it again.

(6) Check to see if it is correct. Repeat the above method until the word is learned.

(7) Ask someone to dictate the entire spelling list while you write the words. Correct them carefully. Study the misspelled words again.

9. Do you improve your study habits in other ways?

a. If you are absent, do you start making up your work as soon as you are able? Use the "buddy system."

b. Do you try to overcome your handicaps in reading, spelling, and multiplication by doing some work on these every day? Remember that if you can multiply well, you can do anything there is to be done in mathematics.

c. Do you have the dictionary habit?

d. Do you try to learn a new word each day?

e. Do you know how to take a test?

f. Do you know how to outline?

g. Do you make full use of the school library?

h. Do you know how to listen attentively and concentrate on what is being said in class?

i. Do you keep notes on what is being said in class? Do you review these notes before an examination?

18. BECOME A PART OF THE GUIDANCE DEPARTMENT

The guidance roles of the school personnel have been neglected by many. The classroom teacher and the homeroom teacher are the most important cogs in the wheels of guidance, since it is from these teachers that the following is gained or directed; it is his personality.

1. *A good self-image.* This comes from positive conditioning, by telling him that he is intelligent, good, that he can do, etc.
2. *Need for feeling personally significant.* Who better can do this? Yes, his parents, but he needs your help.
3. *Discovering of one's identity.* (More difficult for boys) The teacher, the P.E. department, all of the school staff should be a part of this.
4. *Influenced by others.* Understanding of one's susceptibility is a part of knowing one's self.
5. *The loneliness of the child from kindergarten through adolescence.* He needs your love and understanding since you may be the only one who will give it.
6. *The individual differences of all students.*

You as classroom and homeroom teachers must think about these steps and include them in your planning. It would be impossible to develop a positive mind-conditioning program without them.

The classroom teacher must remember that the homeroom teacher can be of great service to him.

19. YOU AND THE READING PROGRAM

The basic emphasis in any program for educating children must revolve around successful instruction in basic reading skills. You, as a teacher, will find it absolutely essential to provide such a program if you are to succeed in all of the other parts of the total training program. Remember that *reading* is essential for all subjects and must be taught as a part of all subjects.

It is unfortunate that many school teachers come to the classroom with little training or background in the "art" of teaching reading. It is hoped that you, as a teacher, are the exception to this rule. If you are not, prepare yourself for the coming challenges by doing some concentrated study to better prepare yourself for the daily tasks that lie ahead. You must train yourself through intensive professional reading, and by the observation of other teachers who are successful in the field of basic reading. Read carefully and critically all that you can find that deals with this most basic of all the teaching processes.

Find out what method your school is using in its reading program. Attempt to see what the professional writer has to offer to the child via your teaching technique. Reading can be taught best by the method which fits your techniques and personality. Read, watch, analyze, and learn all you can. Be prepared to change your belief a dozen times as you try the new ideas. There is a vast difference between reading about a process and utilizing it in a practical sense within the confines of the classroom. Remember, too, that you must have courage and personal enthusiasm for the task. Keep this in mind and you have a fine chance of becoming an excellent teacher of reading or taking care of the reading for your special class such as mathematics, art, English, etc.

Your new class is made up of pupils—human beings—who come to your room from varied backgrounds. Many have been conditioned to hate reading; they have been blocked regarding reading. Some students have been blocked so severely that they cannot see the words. (The same as when a hypnotist tells a subject that a certain person is no longer in the room; however, this person remains and the subject does not see him.) Others become so emotional that they cannot get their eyes to focus, some appear to be normal but cannot seem to remember. All of these students are blocked, induced by someone or by their own thoughts. You must keep telling them to relax, keep telling them you will help them, that you can condition them to learn to read, that it will be easy and fun. Let them know the reason why they are having trouble reading; tell them they are blocked and that you can and will remove the block. You will find that with some pupils picture stories will help to create interest; with others, you will have to use the tracing skills, etc. Be thankful, however, that the percentage of students in such a position is small. For the rest of the students, you will need to use whatever method that seems to work best; you will find that no one method will work with them all. (Be wary of any training method that claims to be a panacea for all reading conditions.) For the top group, or gifted, work on speed and comprehension. However, the slow readers need your skills to help them to understand. These are the students you must reach, but you must not look upon them as mere statistics on a printed page. They are individuals with specific reading disabilities who deserve the best you can offer them in the way of reading encouragement and instruction.

It is your job to develop instructional aids that will help in correcting the disability. Remember that the slow student is blocked, and that each has a different block caused by different conditioning. The student will assist you in every way and will give you complete support and enthusiasm if you work on a positive basis. Support him; develop as much enthusiasm as you can. This will help the slow, the average, and the gifted.

The student must be made to feel and know that you are interested, that you care about him and his problems in reading, writing, listening, and speaking. He must feel that you are there to help him. This is your opportunity to "sell" your reading program and to influence him. If you can do an impressive job of selling at the beginning you have won the first battle but not the war.

After a few class sessions you will soon discover that you have a wide range of reading abilities and interests within your class. You must make some provisions for meeting the varied needs of the students by planning for grouping within your class. This is the only practical and reliable approach if the class is strictly a reading class. However, if it is, say, mathematics, grouping would not have to be but in many cases would be the best. Standardized tests may and do help, but exams and tests devised by the classroom teacher are more practical and reliable. The reasons are, they are more flexible and useful for making quick determinations of an individual's reading ability. This is done by utilizing lists of basic sight vocabulary words as a means of testing. Such a list of words will give you a quick measure of what the child does or does not know in regard to sight vocabulary recognition.

You should use a variety of graded elementary texts to further determine the logical grade placement of the individual student. His personal mannerisms are worth watching and evaluating, in both oral and silent reading.

I would strongly suggest that you read critically all of the professional texts that deal with the teaching of basic reading. They have much to offer the concerned teacher of all classes. Remember to keep telling them that reading is easy. Praise them for good work; practice and be sure mistakes are corrected, since the computer you are programming must have the real facts programmed upon it.

Once you have made a general diagnosis of the reading abilities and disabilities of the entire class and have determined what the approximate reading levels of the group are, you should make plans for meeting the individual needs of the group, and also of the student. Small groups with approximate reading level are the best for you will have a better opportunity to concentrate your remedial measures upon the specific reading disabilities of each individual.

It is well that you know each student's hearing ability. Some students have a hearing loss that will keep them from hearing the words pronounced as they should be; others have not been trained to listen properly.

It might be well at this point for the teacher to adopt the positive resolution, never to be broken, that all of the students in class (whether reading, English, etc.) be obligated to have a reading book in the classroom at all times. It should be expected that the personal reading book will be used during any period of time after class work has been completed. In the upper grades, it is well to have students read and explain their work such as in mathematics, science, shops of all kinds, etc. All upper grades should have word lists for meaning and spelling and should have spelling lessons when the list builds to ten words.

A child learns words and how to read and use these words best by having cards (3 x 5); write and print the words, use them in sentences, spell them, speak them, and re-write them. After reading them, the ones they missed are replaced in a box or group for the next day's lesson. Each student should have his own group of cards to work with.

20. ALL TEACHERS SHOULD

A. Make lesson plans for a day or so ahead of time, so you can think about what you are going to teach, so you can be sure you have the equipment needed to teach this unit or the assignment, so you can be thinking of how best to present a positive lesson on the subject. Also, keep in mind that you must review and cover things you feel were not presented well enough and how to improve upon the last presentation.

B. You should practice and practice how best to condition yourself to positive conditioning, how best to break the negative habits and become very aware of everything you say and do.

C. Things to practice.

1. Smile.
2. A low voice.
3. Don't be overly emotional.
4. Temper control.
5. Think you feel good.
6. Think you enjoy this class.
7. Think yo uenjoy working with and teaching children.
8. Think you want to be a positive teacher.
9. Think you are a good teacher.
10. Think how you think a teacher should think.
11. Think you want to improve as a teacher.
12. Think you are doing something for someone else.

13. Think of new ways to make your positive statements.

14. Think that you will never talk about a student and get yourself and your mind in a dither.

15. Think of more ways to say what you just said or thought.

24. GETTING ALONG WITH OTHERS

1. Learn to make everyone feel that they are important and appreciated.
2. Learn to smile and be cheerful.
3. Learn to cooperate full heartedly.
4. Learn to take care of problems *at once* and not keep other people waiting.
5. Remember the family, their likes and dislikes, their hobbies.
6. Show respect for others, their knowledge and opinions.
7. Learn to respect the right of others.
8. Learn to listen more and talk less.
9. Learn to explain everything that you cover in class.
10. Learn to explain in a positive method.
11. Learn to criticize in a positive way by doing it in between compliments.
12. Learn to remember names and to pronounce them correctly.
13. Keep a seating chart and rearrange your room often.
14. Avoid arguments of all kinds.
15. Don't be afraid to *admit* you are wrong if you are.
16. Learn that good discipline is not harsh and be sure that the student knows why you took action.
17. Learn to be looking for ways to improve your class at all times through

A. Better presentation.
B. By use of better materials.
C. The best motivation for this class.

18. Learn to keep your material on file in such a way that you can find and use it when you need it.

19. See to it that every student in your class is successful.

20. Learn to compliment your students.

22. YOU AND POSITIVE DISCIPLINE

A series of ideas that will help you and the students have a better day if you will practice them.

It is most important for all teachers to remember that positive teaching means positive discipline as well. Students must be taught positive discipline of their minds and their actions. However, through positive mind conditioning and positive thinking the problems of discipline lessen. Students and teachers become enthusiastic about the subject, and as time goes on discipline problems become fewer.

You as teachers must remember that you are changing their way of thinking from negative to positive, their way of acting from bad to good, and that you are conditioning their minds (computers). You also must remember these minds have been conditioned at home, in school, and in the community with a great amount of negative thinking. Here is where you have the chance to influence their thinking. You can keep them from thinking they are dumb, ordinary, selfish, small, below average, malevolent, fools, imps, gangsters, tough (inferiority complex) while they are in your class.

Research has shown that a child will not be damaged in a negative way if he realizes what he has done wrong, why he is being punished and that punishment is not too harsh. Punishment must be fair and just; he must have a way to save face, ways to work himself out of the situation he has created.

Teachers must be all things to the student and must condition *themselves to meet the disciplinary conditions.* A good teacher will develop the personality and mind (computer) of his students to respond to the environment of the class and *will create their class environment.* The following is a list of things a teacher should read every few days; review them until you are reacting with them in your class. At first, this may seem impossible, but as you condition yourself to and with them you will find it can and is done, since most of them are interrelated.

Remember that you can develop the technique of good discipline, good conversation, and can build the self-confidence and the poise you need. You will find you can influence others simply by what you say and how you say it.

Most teachers forget how many different ways they as individuals can encourage and give guidance, self reliance, understanding, and personal concern to the life of someone else. It is your unselfish acts, your personal honesty, your companionship, your truly relaxed gestures that create their mutual respect. So much of the time it is not what you say but how you say it, how you urge them, the initiative you take when you recognize an opening to fill a basic need. Remember that this is not an act of coddling them; it is an act of mind conditioning, it is an art that you can develop. Teaching is an art; it comes from a real desire to help someone develop his talents and to open the way to success.

Usually, when we talk to some great personality about his success, we find that his talents and character took shape from the concern of a teacher who helped him just when he needed it most.

So many teachers feel that what they do in the class to help the individual student is not important; they do not use their opportunity to influence or to respond to extraordinary demands of the student; *self concern rules actions.* It is not for you to build your image; you must help to build the image of the student. Build his self-image and your image will be a part of him; your presence and concern cannot be replaced. You will also be able to overcome inhibitions that have prevented you from being a good teacher, a positive teacher, and you will develop an increased ability to influence the actions and decisions of your students.

Here then, if you are willing to give the following pages earnest study and to practice the principles they explain in your classroom, is a road leading to increased teaching achievement, with unexpected pleasure and at times entertainment.

23. YOU AND YOUR DISCIPLINE

A series of good ideas that will help you to have a better day.

1. See everything; be alert. Employ a wide attention range; be active.

2. Walk around, talk to individuals; *smile* at pupils; ask them pleasant questions to which they can give pleasant answers. Do not be too obvious in your motives.

3. Cultivate and use your sense of humor; not the broad-joke type, but the high-laughter type.

4. Treat each pupil as if he were the mayor's son or daughter; be more than usually courteous to your attendance law prisoners.

5. Make a seating chart and have an information card for each pupil; know names, hobbies, interests, domestic habits. Find out these things by talking informally, subtly, recording the information later.

6. Learn to act sincerely and well. You will have to be stern, happy, firm, informal, kindly, unrelenting, etc. To protect the integrity of your own emotional pattern, learn to act appropriately and sincerely.

7. Be self-confident. Have courage, moral courage to face the situation. It may be hard to appear self-confident, but it is the first essential. These things will help; prepared plans; recreation in nonschool circles; using pupils to help with attendance, books, bulletin board, committees, etc. *If you can't* "TAKE IT," *look for a more pleasant occupation.*

8. See your pupils somewhere else in the school; on

the athletic field; on the playground at noon; at student council; at school parties, etc.

9. Keep an adult reserve of formality which the pupils know is there; no playing for popularity, no siding with pupils against other teachers or administration; with the students, never of them; no favorites or crushes; always Miss, Mrs., or Mr., never just Smith.

10. Be just and very fair. Put yourself in the pupil's place. The Golden Rule. What shape would you be in without sleep, food, or security?

11. In disciplinary situations, suspend your judgment; often be impersonal, sometimes even coldly nonchalant. It is not necessary to settle every case. You are dealing with the *psychology,* not the *logic* of the situation.

12. Say so when you are in error; even be ready to apologize, but not too often.

13. Be enthusiastic about your subject, and it will kindle response in your pupils.

14. Do nothing yourself that you can get the pupils to do, even though they do it less effectively. The schooling is for them; they like to help.

15. Encourage rather than scold when pupils do poorly. There is usually something you can compliment, even a sharp pencil or well combed hair.

16. Create a learning emergency in which you share a problem with them; the pupils like nothing better; e.g. "what shall we do about this?"

17. Try never to become angry; too active adrenals mean mental confusion; lower your voice, grow impassive, but avoid a scene; after all, it is a professional, not a personal matter.

18. Do everything you can to build up the ego of each pupil; job, honors, a kindly compliment, a smile all count more in the pupils' lives than we realize.

19. Use your voice effectively; it can soothe when lowered, create enthusiasm when the tones are rich and the

range of pitch is wide; it can accentuate bedlam when it tries to outshout it.

20. Every once in a while do something for the class yourself with an air that you are happy to please them. Be an actor; use your voice, your poise and act. Read to them, show them a clipping, tell an interesting personal experience—all to make them feel cared for.

21. Try to avoid creating situations where pupils have to lie. Above all, let them save face when you know they are in a tight spot. You be an *actor.*

22. Teach them something; they really want it. Have something ready for them.

23. Make an interesting environment of the room with the help of the pupils. Have good magazines about, books with attractive jackets, pictures, etc.

24. Encourage pupils to have a library book to fill spare moments or to relieve the strain of working too long on one thing.

25. Never lecture; discuss with them, but *never lecture.* Remember your faculty-meeting experiences, your dad, or your teachers. Se how little you can talk out loud to the whole class. Get in your "licks" by talking quietly to individuals.

26. When you are uncertain what to do about a class situation or an individual case, simply ask yourself what common sense would suggest. You will be surprised at the simplicity of the solution.

27. When you give directions, let them be clear and concise; say them out loud, distinctly, while you look into a selection of pupils' eyes; write them out, understanding that they read them, underlining with yellow chalk the parts to be noted particularly; then ask several pupils to tell what they mean. Take nothing for granted. Above all ask, "and why are we doing this?" If there is no intelligent answer, select a different task.

28. Have your plans ready when the class starts. Never tie yourself up by having to put material on the board

during class time. Pupils will do it while you are circulating.

29. If you are in the school for the first time and perhaps just for the day, make a quick survey of the educational flavor of the place; there are ways to tell; the initial office greeting, the books in the teachers' library, the decorations, the restrooms and the lunchroom talk; say little, observe carefully.

30. If a new class stages "a tempest in a teacup," sit down with them, drop your own book; laugh with them and say you get paid for it. Take the matter lightly in stride and they will soon swear by you. Better than glaring and fear. Keep "twenty jumps" ahead of the students.

31. When you have *put a class to work,* avoid *interrupting* them by across-the-room comments to individuals. Leave them alone; pupils find constant interruptions by teachers distracting.

32. Make a check list of disciplinary measures that should be exhausted before sending the "case pupil" to the office; for example:

a.—give interesting work to do.

b.—talk to him.

c.—take away privileges but leave a way out for him.

d.—see him after school.

e.—check with his homeroom teacher.

f.—exercise the brute by sending him on an errand or asking the physical education instructor to permit an additional workout.

g.—have him write an agreement which he must get the homeroom teacher and vice-principal to sign—also, perhaps, his parents.

h.—write a note to his parents; phone them; ask them to visit his class or you; visit his home.

i.—get all personal data from the counselor and homeroom teacher.

j.—go with him to vice-principal for conference; send

him to the principal's office; do something nice to show no ill will.

k.—be sure he understands the reason for every move you make.

33. Never scare pupils by telling them how hard a subject is (don't try to build up your ego this way). Tell them instead, how easy it was for you.

34. Prove to them that the subject you teach is easy.

35. Convince them how smart they are and discuss their great abilities.

36. Help them; explain, and explain why.

37. Believe in your subject and your work; show them that you enjoy the subject. Influence them, sell them.

38. Remember that at home these students are exposed to all the negative conditioning they can take.

39. Don't ever say: "I think you will like this." Say, instead, like a salesman: "You will like this," or like a hypnotist: "You are getting sleepy." Say "You *are* going to like this; it will be easy and fun to do."

24. SOME GOOD METHODS OF LEARNING TO READ

The Fernald Method

For the remedial student and at times for the slow reader.

Stage I. Tracing.

A. The child is motivated in two ways; first he is told that he may try a new method of learning words that is very easy and works with everyone; second, he is encouraged to learn "any words he wishes to use but does not know how to write."

B. The teacher writes the words with chalk or crayon on a large card or piece of paper while the child observes the process. Either manuscript or cursive writing is used, but manuscript is preferred because it more nearly approximates the printed word in a book. A reading program should be conducted when the child is relaxed without pressure. If he is upset make an attempt to set another time.

C. The child traces the word with his finger until he can reproduce it correctly without looking at the copy. (With some people the mind is programmed best when both physical and mental processes are working at the same time.)

1. The child traces with his first and second fingers. (Tracing with chalk, crayon, pencil, or stylus does not produce the desired results.) As he traces, he says the word by parts.

2. The child says the word by syllables in a natural tone as he writes each part. This writing is first done on scrap paper before putting it in a story on record.

3. The word is written without looking at the copy. If an error is made, the whole word is traced again and again until it can be written without looking at the copy. Attention is directed to the correct form, not the errors.

4. The whole word is written without looking at the copy. The word is always written as a unit.

A person's nervous system is coordinated with his mind; thus the nerves in his hands, arms and fingers are coordinated with his mind, and to trace with his fingers reinforces the act.

D. The word is always used in context. During the first few periods, the word may not be used in a story. The purpose of the initial activities is to convince the child that he can learn words and that he can remember them. However; the word must have meaning to the child. It must be one which he is interested in learning. After the first period or so, the child learns words by this method which he wishes to use in a story or some type of experience record. He may ask for words to label pictures in booklets or for stories.

E. After the child completes a story or record, the teacher types it immediately so that it can be read in print.

F. After the labeling of the story is complete, the child files the words learned in alphabetical order.

G. Frequent checks on retention are made. Rereading labels and stories, as well as flash-cards, are used as a means of appraising retention.

H. During stage one, the child makes use of several aids to learning. First, the word has meaning to the child, he is motivated by a desire to use the word for communication; second, the child sees the word written by the teacher, he sees it as he traces, he sees it as he writes, and he sees it in final typed form; third, by using direct finger contact in tracing, the child feels the word as he says and sees it; fourth, by arm movement in tracing and writing the word, the child feels the word as he says and sees it; fifth, by pronouncing the word as he traces and writes it, the child feels the word with his speech apparatus; sixth, by hearing the word pronounced, the child is given an additional aid for retention. When all these methods of learning are used, the child should learn to read.

I. How long a child stays in stage one depends on the degree of his handicap. Some complete this stage in a few days, some in two or three months, and others will take a year.

J. The child is given no systematic help in phonetic analysis at this time. The emphasis is on structural analysis, especially syllabification.

Stage II. Writing from script.

A. Stage one has been achieved when words can be learned without tracing. The need for tracing is reduced gradually. That is, the number of retracings required to learn a word is reduced until tracing is no longer necessary. In short, tracing is discontinued when the child can learn without it.

B. The child learns a word by looking at the word in script, by saying it, and by writing it without a copy as he says each part.

1. The child identifies the word he cannot write.

2. The teacher writes it in small script, pronouncing each part. The word is written as a whole. A small card (perhaps (3 X 5) is used in this stage.

3. If some tracing is necessary at the beginning of this stage, the child says each part of the word as he traces it. It is important that the word be spoken as in conversa-

tion; no distortion of the sounds of letters or syllables is permitted.

4. The child says each part of the word as he writes it, without the copy.

5. The word is always written as a whole by the child. When an error is made, the child either retraces or looks at it (saying it to himself) until he can write it without copy.

C. The child's composition is typed immediately by the teacher.

D. The child reads the typed copy without delay; silent reading is used to prepared for fluent oral reading.

E. When tracing is not necessary, small cards (3 X 5) are used and filed in a small box.

F. No attempt is made to simplify the vocabulary, sentence structure, or concepts in the child's composition. The learning and retention of larger words are, in general, better than that of shorter words.

G. Immediate and delayed recall is checked with the flash cards from the small file box.

H. The only mode of learning eliminated in this stage is that of tracing.

Stage III. Writing from print (Initial book reading).

A. This stage has been reached when the child can write the word after looking at it in printed form. It is no longer necessary for the teacher to write the word for him. Instead, she pronounces it to and for the child. (When a child reaches this stage, the teacher must make a big thing of it. Parents must be told, other students of the class must be told and there should be a new privilege that goes with this accomplishment.)

1. The child looks at the word and says it to himself.

2. The child writes the word from memory, that is, without looking at the copy.

3. If the child is unable to make the transfer from print to script, the teacher writes the word for the child. The child then writes the word and identifies it in print.

B. At this stage, the child begins to read from books.

1. Silent reading is always done first.

2. During silent reading, unknown words are identified and the child is told what they are.

3. After the silent reading is completed, the "new" words are learned by first looking at the printed word and then writing it without looking at it.

C. Immediate and delayed recall of words is appraised by using flash cards or some other means.

Stage IV. Recognition of words without writing (Book reading and visual analysis techniques.)

A. This stage has been reached when it is no longer necessary for the child to write a word in order to remember it. As he looks at the word, the simultaneous association by similarity with words he already knows, together with the meaning inferred from the context, gives him an instant perception of the word.

B. Phrasing is improved by developing the habit of silent reading to clear up the meaning of the new words.

C. During this procedure the fourth stage of progress is rapid.

D. With this procedure, children always do their own reading; no one ever reads to them (as a part of their reading lesson).

E. Word recognition is developed by a syllabification approach. Writing the word without copy is used when necessary.

1. Words are never spelled orally.

2. Words are always written as a whole, never in separated syllables.

3. The child never copies the word, it is always written from memory.

4. The correct form of the word is emphasized; the incorrect form (an error) is always erased or covered up.

It is our wish to emphasize that there are many methods of teaching reading, that no one method is the answer to all reading problems. Therefore, you will find it practical to use parts, stages, etc. of methods you study and learn to use.

25. THE BASAL READER METHOD

The child learns to read in a graded series of increasingly difficult books. These books repeat the words to be learned many times and introduce only about two new words per page so that there is a gradual and controlled growth of vocabulary and complexity of sentence structure.

A Combination of Practical Techniques for Teaching Reading

1. Determine the reading grade level of the child from written and oral tests.
2. Begin with an interesting book or selection on his level and interest.
3. As the child reads, tell him words he doesn't know, meanwhile printing or writing them in a list.
4. When he finishes reading the selection in the book, ask him to read to you the list of words which you made as he read. (If you think he doesn't know the meaning of the word, ask him to use it illustratively in a sentence. If he can't, you tell him the meaning and use it in a sentence.)
5. If he does not remember the word, ask him to look at it carefully and then write it from memory three to five times as necessary.
6. If he still does not remember the word, write it for him to trace until he learns it.
7. Keep the list of words he missed in a notebook for reviews.

8. When you are not working individually with the child, he may be kept profitably busy by the following activities;

a. Put the words from his list into sentences.

b. Alphabetize the words from his list and divide them into syllables.

c. Write the words in lower case letters and then with an initial capital letter to see the difference in the appearance.

d. Illustrate the words with drawings or collected pictures.

When to Break the Rule

9. In helping the child figure out words in his reading, it is all right to give the child occasional helpful explanations on syllabification and the sounds of letters so long as you still hold the interest of the child. (Most authorities say that this help should be given outside the regular reading situation.) Phonetics are important, but in most cases not to the degree that they distract the pupil from a story. Phonetics should come more in the spelling lessons than reading.

10. Continue to increase the child's reading ability through help on the three basic reading skills: vocabulary development, comprehension, and speed.

There are many good ways to teach reading, literature, spelling, and all the related reading lessons. Therefore, you as the teacher should use the method that fits your salesmanship ability. You should also remember that some learn best with one method, and others with parts of other methods mixed together, etc. However, whatever method you use, be sure to motivate the student, be sure that all negative conditioning has been eliminated from the method before you begin. It is better not to start a reading lesson if an emotional situation prevails. More students are blocked in their reading process than in any other subject. Pressure becomes negative with so many students. Students who read well, do well in school; teach them to read well and the rest of their school work will follow.

26. FOR THE PARENTS

If I should close this book without advice to the parents, on how to condition their children, I would be doing a great injustice. Conditioning the mind begins with the small child. A baby can be motivated to be happy, to smile, to coo, or he can be motivated to fear at a very early age. Therefore, mind conditioning begins very early in life.

Children are born with many intuitions; none or very few of these are negative. Negative reasonings are induced. A child has a drive to achieve success. He will spend hours encountering an obstacle, days of practice to accomplish or master a feat. Success drives him on to other accomplishments. He has pride in his achievements.

This pride in achievement, or drive to reach new plateaus is a pleasure to him. This pleasure will continue if he is encouraged. Children find enjoyment and delight in this success, and even more so when they are urged to be successful.

However, the inner drive of a child can be changed from pleasure to hate, to fear, with all the great motivating force drained from his with only a very few negative senseless remarks or actions, such as punishment or disapproval.

The kind of punishment and disapproval has a great deal to do with the kind of reaction or response the child will show. The understanding of such punishment and disapproval of adults by the child is important and should not be a forced conditioning.

The cause of punishment or a show of disapproval by adults to children's actions in most cases *is due to the fact that the things he does are troublesome to the adult* or an inconvenience to him. Seldom does the adult consider how the child feels or what caused him to do what he did.

If your child is doing something that is an inconvenience to you or against your wishes, guide him and encourage him to do something else that you can praise him for. Parents are teachers, and it is their job to teach their children the things they wish them to do. Remember, teaching is accomplished best when the child is relaxed, when he has been motivated to react. A parent must be very careful never to damage the inner drive of a child by undue pressure. Your child may not be conditioned to respond to your plan; therefore, it is up to you to plan more motivation and conditioning to accomplish what you had in mind.

Whatever your plans are to motivate your child into doing, be sure he can or should be able to do the act. Don't ever try to motivate a child into an act or start him trying to accomplish an act that is impossible for him. Remember that failures become negative if you are not careful.

When a father of eleven children was interviewed on Art Linkletter's program and was asked, "How do you discipline a family of eleven?" I was very pleased with his answer, which was, "We just keep them happy and busy." I wonder if you realize what a problem this must be with a family of eleven children. However, I wish you could have met these children so that you could see the wonderful gleam in their eyes, their wonderful manners, and respectful deportment.

The answer, "We just keep them happy and busy," means more than first meets the mind. To keep them happy called for positive conditioning and for fairness in punishment. "We keep them happy and busy." The art of keeping children busy is important, and keeping them both happy and busy is even more important.

Parents should study their child, they should keep a

record on what he *likes* and *dislikes,* what motivates him most, and keep records of any changes that occur. Most personality and character qualities are developed at home, his talents depend on the mind conditioning received in the home first and then in the school. The early years are the formative years, the years when his success or failure are largely determined.

As I mentioned before, toys are not the answer. Toys should be interesting and challenging to the child. Parents should help their child learn to use the toy. Praise and a pat on the back are the important motivation he needs to continue his efforts. As he grows and develops, new and more challenging activities should be ready for him. Keep the child feeling good about himself, feeling happy about *your helping* him master his problems, do your best to keep the joy of being busy with a constructive activity going every day.

As the child grows older, let him choose the activity more and more. There should be picture books at a very early age, even before he can turn the pages. This is when you should talk to him about the pictures as you turn the pages, tell stories about them, and let him turn the pages by holding the page so he can do so.

Put the book in with his toys in order that he may look at it as he finds time. At an early age start reading and telling stories about things that he sees and hears, even before he is talking a great deal. At first, this activity will be very short-lived but pursue it. His span of attention will lengthen as he matures, and this activity helps him mature. Keep reading to him as he grows older, read the same stories over and over. Let him see the book as you read, and when he begins to ask about words, point them out and explain them to him.

When he can hold a crayon in his hand and make a mark, you should make crayons and paper available to him. Remember now that you are the teacher. Teach him to make lines, to make X's, etc., and then let him color the paper as he sees fit. Pictures will be an early activity for him, letters and words will follow, as he starts to school and in many cases long before. Printing his name should be learned before school begins and at times much earlier, but don't let this become a "must" with you. Let him grow and mature at this without pressure or punishment; let it be a successful experience. Reading to a child should continue up to or beyond the fourth grade. Helping him read depends on his desire to read and that comes from your reading to him.

Motivating a child to read works best if the parent conditions the student. Reading readiness comes from the conditioning a student has received at home or at school, but he should have been so conditioned before the first grade.

Sometimes the things not to do are more important than those that should be done. I am sure you can make a list of things not to do after reading this book. You can plan your reading readiness program from the information it contains, and you can program your teaching chores on a very positive basis. Teaching is indicative of positive mind conditioning, not negative.

Parents quite often say to me, "You can't tell me I am negative; we love our children and want only the best for them." Teachers quite often will challenge me to show them why I think that they are using a lot of negative conditioning in their classes. I wish to point out that negative conditioning has been a common practice. Almost everyone teaches as he has been taught to teach. This fact was brought out to me by a teacher quite some years ago.

This teacher (I will call him Joe) challenged me to prove to him that he was conditioning his students negatively. This happened a few days before the end of the first semester. I knew that he had an English class the next semester when I had a free period. I asked Joe if he cared if I visited this class of his the first day of the semester, and he welcomed me to do so.

I was amazed to hear him welcome his new students with the following. "Students, this class deals with a subject very few students or adults are capable of mastering. English is hard to learn. No one in this class has the ability to earn an 'A' grade. I flunk over one-third of my students, so you are going to have to study hard each day to even keep up with the class. You have to study harder in an English class to learn it than in any other class. You will have to study at least two hours a day if you plan to keep up." At this point I got up and walked out. I knew the rest of his speech by heart for I had heard it over and over years before when I was a student. I made a copy of what I heard Joe say, then I included the rest by saying, "Joe, I know you went ahead and said this." I put this copy in Joe's mail box at school so he could see for himself before I talked to him about it. You're right; Joe saw that he was conditioning his students to be afraid of English and also of him, their teacher. He came to me and asked, "How can I overcome this?"

Joe was teaching as he was taught. Parents teach as they were taught. Students respond as they are taught. This vicious circle must be broken; mind conditioning must be understood and used by parents, teachers, and students.

Some of the things that parents do so often (in most homes) is to constantly tell their child "No!" No!" or "Stop that!" without doing anything about putting him to work at something constructive. Children should be told why they should not do whatever they are doing that is wrong.

Many parents belittle their child in front of others, spank him at the drop of the hat, and some set up a punishment so rigid that the child can never work himself out of the restrictions.

I wish to repeat that I am not against discipline; however, the chastisement must be explained and he must be able to clear himself without a great emotional disorder.

Most students who are conditioned negatively have the feeling of being unwanted; they feel that they are inferior in all ways, that they are not a part of anything. They need love and understanding before they will change their way of thinking.

Most delinquent students have lost their feeling for values. Very few have a feeling toward God or an inner feeling of any kind, let alone a feeling of success.

Dr. Stafford Warren, who was the special advisor to the President of the United States on mental retardation, said, "A large percentage of the nation's five and one half million retarded have low I.Q.'s simply because they never had any mental stimulation during the years their brains were developing." I wish to add that they were also conditioned negatively.

BOOK CATALOG

New! HYPNOTISM AND MYSTICISM OF INDIA

By Ormond McGill
Dean of American Hypnotists;
author of *"Professional Stage Hypnotism."*

Now you can learn ***ORIENTAL HYPNOTISM*** as performed by the Masters of India; there are their secret teachings. Noted author and hypnotist Ormond McGill reveals how the real mysticism and magic of India is accomplished. You are taught how to be adept.

The original draft of this book was written in Calcutta in collaboration with the great Hindu Sage, Sadhu Parimal Bandu . . . it may well be called the "textbook" of the Hindu Hypnotists and Magicians, and reveals secrets that have been closely guarded for centuries and known only to the limited view. Now **these secrets can be yours.** Note the remarkable Table of Contents of subjects covered in depth so you can now perform the mysticism and magic of India:

Hindu Fakir Magic, Genuine East Indian Magic, The Science of Pranayama, Oriental Rhythmic Breathing Techniques, Yogi Pranayama Practices, The Mastery of the Mind, The Power of Concentration, Oriental Vizualization and Projection, The Magic Power of Words and Sound, Learning the Art of Maya, Occidental/Oriental Hypnotism, Silent Psychic Influence, Yogi Mental Broadcasting, The Psychic Control of Events, The Magic of Love, The Secrets of Yoga Cosmology, Becoming a Master Magician and Hypnotist, Yama, Yogi Self-Development, The Great "I AM," Index.

You are instructed exactly as the Hindu magicians and hypnotists themselves are instructed, showing you exactly how to develop these remarkable powers. Included are detailed instructions in Oriental Hypnotism which is the finest method of hypnotizing ever developed—combining both Oriental and Occidental techniques. You are shown the Yogi Art of Maya for hypnotically controlling the minds of others. How to Read the Akashic Records, Astral Projection, Yoga Cosmology, and how to perform Yama, the Yoga Method of Self-Hypnosis that can make a man over completely anew.

Limited First Edition – deluxe and hardbound, with dust jacket – 208 pages – fully illustrated – $10.95

Best Seller!

SELF HYPNOSIS And Other Mind Expanding Techniques

BROUGHT TOGETHER FOR THE FIRST TIME: Techniques and How-to of Self-hypnosis, Auto-suggestion, Behavior Modification, Faith Healing and Subconscious Reprogramming

---

By Charles Tebbetts

Much of the material in this book, theoretical as well as practical, was stimulated by the remarkable teachings and influence of an extraordinary man, Gil Boyne, a certified Hypnotherapist who has a Hypnotism Institute just off the campus of U.C.L.A.

I began my studies with Gil Boyne in 1970 and I was quickly captivated by his charisma and personal power. I always had the sense of watching a gifted artist at work when I watched him induce a hypnotic trance in a matter of seconds. I have never seen anyone induce hypnosis as fast as Gil Boyne does. By the end of the course I could hypnotize myself and program my deeper mind in minutes.

Mr. Boyne calls his method of overcoming the negative scripts of the past, "POWER PROGRAMMING"! He has revised the stereotyped concepts of Auto-suggestion and created the first totally new methods in more than forty years!

Gil Boyne teaches his methods to capacity classes five nights a week, and in the many classes I attended I met an extraordinary cross-section of humanity, ranging from aspiring performers to celebrated super-stars and athletes, from bank tellers to corporation presidents. Some of the people I met at Gil Boyne's Self-Help Institute are: commedienne Lily Tomlin; National Bowling Champion Barry Asher; Sylvester Stallone, writer and star of the film "Rocky"; the charismatic TV minister Reverend Ike; Lloyd Haines, TV star of "Room 222"; Lisa Todd of TV's "Hee Haw"; film and TV star Sheree North; famed concert violinist Endre Balogh; writer Jane Wagner (writer-producer for Lily Tomlin). In short, all kinds of people from all walks of life come to study with the man whose methods I described in this book.

Third Edition – 128 pages – softbound – $3.95

You Can Activate the Power of Your Subconscious Mind and...
COME ALIVE!
with SELF HYPNOSIS and "POWER PROGRAMMING"
by Gil Boyne
Authority on Hypnosis Motivation and Mental Programming

CASSETTE TAPE #101 — SELF-CONFIDENCE THROUGH SELF-IMAGE PROGRAMMING
Radiate dynamic self-confidence — Improve your self-image — Overcome the fear of criticism, fear of rejection, fear of failure — Feel more lovable and appreciate yourself more **$9.95**

CASSETTE TAPE #102 — CONCENTRATION — MEMORY — RETENTION — PERFECT RECALL
This method is the only scientifically-validated memory system known — requires no memorization of key words or word associations — liberate your photographic memory — a fool-proof cure for forgetfulness — use your automatic mind search and memory-scanning capacity. The unique methods are placed indelibly into your subconscious mind for your permanent use. **$9.95**

CASSETTE TAPE #103 — DEEP RELAXATION AND RESTFUL SLUMBER
Here is a new way to go to sleep! This incredibly effective and totally safe technique enables you to shed the cares of the day and drift off within minutes after your head hits the pillow. Your float into a sleep as refreshing and rejuvenating as it is deep. You feel new vitality and energy each morning, and you maintain high energy levels through the day. **$9.95**

CASSETTE TAPE #104 — SECRETS OF SUCCESS ATTITUDES
Overcomes your subconscious "will to fail" — you can learn to move rapidly toward your career and financial goals — success and riches spring from a foundation of "subconscious mental expectancy" — money does not come from high IQ, education, hard work or goodness — begin now to realize the enduring success and wealth that is potentially yours! **$9.95**

CASSETTE TAPE #105 — TRIM AND FIT — VITAL AND HEALTHY
The mental factors in compulsive overeating are widely recognized. This new method conditions your nervous system and your subconscious mind to rapidly move you toward your goal of attractive fitness. Gives you a new self image about your physical self. Changes your eating habits by changing your appetite desires. Improves your figure easily and quickly. **$9.95**

CASSETTE TAPE #106 — SECRETS OF COMMUNICATION AND EXPRESSION
How to present your ideas in a way that insures acceptance. If you are the one who feels fear and tension at the thought of having to give a speech or a short report, this tape is a blessing! You can speak with absolute confidence and perfect poise, whether to an audience of hundreds or a small group or a single person. **$9.95**

CASSETTE TAPE #107 — DYNAMICS OF CREATIVE ACTING
Program your mind for success in your acting career. Covers auditions, rehearsing, performing, mental attitude and self-image. Overcome, "The Freeze," learn lines quickly and easily. Express your creativity. **$9.95**

CASSETTE TAPE #108 — DYNAMICS OF SELF-DISCOVERY
Answers the question, "WHO AM I?"! Overcomes the identity crisis. Creates a powerful belief in your own abilities. Discover the real self and your true capacity for joyful living! Teaches you how to give yourself — love, acceptance and approval. **$9.95**

CASSETTE TAPE #109 – DYNAMIC HEALTH AND RADIANT VITALITY
You can overcome fears and negative beliefs and your state of health. This program subconsciously develops the mental imagery, feeling tone, and mental expectancy for radiant, vibrant expression of perfect health.

CASSETTE TAPE #112 — DYNAMICS OF CREATIVE WRITING
The hypnotic programming tape that was developed for a producer-writer of a famous dramatic-comedy T.V. show. This writer later claimed that this programming was an important factor in the creation of a script that won an Emmy nomination. **$9.95**

NEW **CASSETTE TAPE #114 — YOU CAN STOP SMOKING NOW!**
This power-programmed cassette will overcome the helpless feeling that underlies tobacco addiction. In just a short time, you become free of tobacco -- permanently! Enjoy a longer, healthier, happier life. **$9.95**

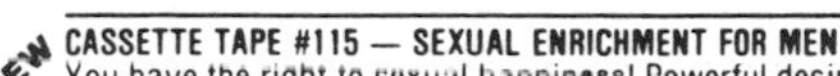
NEW **CASSETTE TAPE #115 — SEXUAL ENRICHMENT FOR MEN**
You have the right to sexual happiness! Powerful desire, total function, and glowing fulfillment is the result of your use of this program. **$9.95**

NEW **CASSETTE TAPE #116 — SEXUAL ENRICHMENT FOR WOMEN**
See description above for #115. **$9.95**